LOMA's GLOSSARY of Insurance Terms
Third Edition

Edited by

Nicholas L. Desoutter, FLMI, ACS
and Kenneth Huggins, FLMI/M

2300 Windy Ridge Parkway
Atlanta, Georgia 30339-8443

T0204257

Project Team:

Project Editor	Nicholas L. Desoutter, FLMI, ACS
Managing Editor	Elizabeth A. Mulligan, FLMI, ACS, AIAA, ALHC
Project Manager	Katherine C. Milligan, FLMI, ALHC
Cover Design	Zoila Harmouche
Production	Cara Taylor Gaskins
	Denise Dorage Wagner

LOMA (Life Office Management Association) is an international association founded in 1924. LOMA's mission is to help member companies in the insurance and financial services industry improve their management and operations through quality employee development, research, information sharing, and related products and services. Among LOMA's activities is the sponsorship of the FLMI Insurance Education Program—an educational program intended primarily for home office and branch office employees.

While a great deal of care has been taken to provide accurate, current, and authoritative information in regard to the subject matter covered in this book, the ideas, suggestions, general principles, conclusions, and any other information presented here are for general educational purposes only. This text is sold with the understanding that it is neither designed nor intended to provide the reader with legal, accounting, investment, marketing, or other types of professional business management advice. If legal advice or other expert assistance is required, the services of a competent professional should be sought.

ISBN 1-57974-004-9

Printed in the United States of America

About *LOMA's Glossary* of Insurance Terms

LOMA's Glossary helps to explain the jargon of life insurance, health insurance, and employee benefits. This glossary is intended for the novice and the veteran alike. If you have a question about an insurance term, *LOMA's Glossary* can probably answer it.

With this edition, besides updating many of the terms in the earlier editions, we have expanded *LOMA's Glossary* by more than 200 terms. The glossary now defines terms from practically all the major areas of business in which life and health insurers operate. The new terms were drawn primarily from the areas of insurance accounting, finance, and managed health care. *LOMA's Glossary* now lists and defines more than 1,600 terms that are used in the life and health insurance industry.

We're always looking for new terms and better definitions that will make *LOMA's Glossary* a better and more complete reference for the industry. If you come across a term that is not defined in the glossary, or if you find a definition in the glossary that you think can be improved, please let us know. Send your comments to

LOMA
Insurance & Financial Services Programs
2300 Windy Ridge Parkway, Suite 600
Atlanta, Georgia 30339-8443
Attn: LOMA's Glossary

If you would like to order additional copies of *LOMA's Glossary*, contact:

Professional Book Distributors, Inc. (PBD)
1650 Bluegrass Lakes Parkway
P.O. Box 930108
Atlanta, Georgia 31193-0108
U.S.A.
(800) 887-3723 for placing orders from outside Georgia
(770) 442-8631, Ext. 253 for placing orders from inside Georgia

We look forward to your comments, and we hope you find *LOMA's Glossary* a useful and convenient addition to your insurance library.

Nicholas L. Desoutter, FLMI, ACS
Kenneth Huggins, FLMI/M

Acknowledgements

We would like to express our gratitude to the industry experts who provided invaluable help with the development of this and previous editions of *LOMA's Glossary of Insurance Terms*. These experts made excellent suggestions both for determining appropriate terminology for inclusion in the glossary and for improving the clarity and accuracy of definitions.

Additional Helpful Publications
from LOMA's Education Division

Principles of Insurance: Life, Health, and Annuities (1996),
Harriett E. Jones and Dani L. Long

Principles des assurances de personnes et des rentes (1996), translation of
Principles of Insurance: Life, Health, and Annuities

Operations of Life and Health Insurance Companies, Second Edition
(1992), Kenneth Huggins and Robert D. Land

Exploitation des compagnies d'assurances de personnes, Second Edition
(1993), translation of *Operations of Life and Health Insurance Companies,*
Second Edition

Canadian Life and Health Insurance Law (1992), Harriett E. Jones

Droit des assurances de personnes au Canada (1993), translation of
Canadian Life and Health Insurance Law

Life and Health Insurance Marketing, Second Edition (1998), Sharon B.
Allen, Dennis W. Goodwin, and Jennifer W. Herrod

Le marketing des assurances de personnes (1991)*, translation of Life and
Health Insurance Marketing*

Information Management in Insurance Companies (1995),
Kenneth Huggins, Dani L. Long, and Vicki Mason Pfrimmer

Utilisation de la statistique dans la gestion de l'information (1995),
translation of *Information Management in Insurance Companies*

Accounting and Financial Reporting in Life and Health Insurance
(1997), Elizabeth A. Mulligan and Gene Stone

*Managing for Solvency and Profitability in Life and Health Insurance
Companies* (1996), Susan Conant, Nicholas L. Desoutter, Dani L. Long,
and Robert MacGrogan

Insurance Administration (1997), Jane Lightcap Brown

Intro to Life and Health Insurance: Fundamentals of Insurance Concepts and Products (1997), Nicholas L. Desoutter and Jena L. Kennedy

Intro to Annuities: Fundamentals of Annuity Concepts and Products (1996), Jena L. Kennedy

Intro to Managed Care: Fundamentals of Managed Care Coverage and Providers, Second Edition (1998), Jena L. Kennedy

Customer Service in Insurance: Principles and Practices, Second Edition (1997), Kenneth Huggins, Dani L. Long, and Caroline W. Sundberg

Customer Service in Insurance: Improving Your Skills (1991), Richard Bailey, Kenneth Huggins, and Dani L. Long

LOMA's
Glossary
of Insurance Terms

absolute assignment An assignment of a life insurance policy or annuity contract under which the policyowner or annuity con- tractowner transfers all policy ownership rights to an assignee. See also *assignment* and *collateral assignment.*

accelerated death benefit rider A supplementary life insurance policy benefit rider that allows a policyowner-insured to receive a specified portion of the policy's death benefit before the policyowner insured's death if certain conditions are met. Also known as *living benefit rider.*

accidental death and dismemberment (AD&D) rider A supplementary life insurance policy benefit rider that provides for an amount of money in addition to the basic death benefit of a life insurance policy. This additional amount is payable only if the insured dies or loses any two limbs or the sight of both eyes as the result of an accident. Some AD&D riders pay one half of the benefit amount if the insured loses one limb or the sight in one eye.

accidental death benefit (ADB) rider A supplementary life insurance policy benefit rider that provides for an amount of money in addition to the basic death benefit of a life insurance policy. This additional amount is payable only if the insured dies as the result of an accident.

accidental means provision Alife insurance policy accidental death benefit provision which states that an accidental death benefit will be payable if the insured's death was the result, directly and independently of all other causes, of bodily injury caused solely by external, violent, and accidental means.

accidental result provision A life insurance policy accidental death benefit provision which states that an accidental death benefit will be payable if the insured's death was the result, directly and independently of all other causes, of accidental bodily injury.

accident perils A classification used by health insurance underwriters to evaluate the type and degree of peril represented by a particular occupation. Accident perils include exposure to fire, the use of dangerous machinery, the handling of heavy objects, and the risk of falling. See also *illness perils.*

account See *territory.*

accrual taxation A method of federal income taxation in which the owner of a life insurance policy is taxed periodically on portions of the policy's cash value build-up.

accrued benefit In a defined benefit pension plan, the amount of pension benefit that has accumulated in a pension plan on behalf of an individual plan participant as of a specified date.

accumulated cost of insurance At any time during the life of a block of policies, the amount the insurer has paid in benefits since the beginning of the contract, accumulated at interest. Used to calculate policy reserves by the *retrospective method.*

accumulated funding deficiency In the United States, the amount by which a qualified pension plan fails to meet the minimum funding standards set by law. Plans with an accumulated funding deficiency are subject to a penalty tax and enforcement provisions. Sometimes simply called a *funding deficiency.*

accumulated value The net amount paid by the contract owner for a deferred annuity plus interest earned, less the amount of any withdrawals and fees.

accumulation at interest dividend option A life insurance policy dividend option under which policy dividends are left on deposit with the insurer to accumulate at interest. Also called the *accumulation option.*

accumulation factor The quantity by which an amount of money is multiplied in order to determine the accumulated value of that money after one year. This quantity equals one plus the applicable interest rate.

accumulation option See *accumulation at interest option.*

accumulation period The period between the contractowner's purchase of a deferred annuity and the onset of the annuity's payout period.

accumulation units The term used to identify ownership shares in a variable annuity's separate-account fund. When a person pays premiums for a variable annuity, those premiums are credited to the purchaser's account as a certain number of accumulation units. After the accumulation period ends, the accumulation units are used to buy annuity units. See also *annuity units.*

ACLI See *American Council of Life Insurance (ACLI).*

acquisition expenses See *policy acquisition costs.*

active life reserves Health insurance reserves which, like policy reserves for life insurance, help ensure that an insurer will have sufficient assets to pay future claims.

actively-at-work provision A group insurance contract provision which specifies that, if an employee is absent from work on the day the employee's coverage under the contract is due to begin, then coverage will not begin until the day the employee returns to work.

actuarial assumptions (1) The mortality, morbidity, interest, expense, and other forecasts used to calculate premium rates and reserves. (2) In pension planning, the assumptions that actuaries make in the areas of investment earnings, mortality, plan expenses, salary levels, and employee turnover. These assumptions affect the amount of the annual contribution that is necessary to adequately fund a defined benefit pension plan.

actuarial cost method For a defined benefit pension plan, a method of calculating the annual amount a plan sponsor must contribute to fund a given set of plan benefits for a particular group of participants.

actuarial department The department in a life and health insurance company responsible for seeing that the company's operations are conducted on a mathematically sound basis. In conjunction with other departments, it designs and revises a company's life and health insurance products. The actuarial department calculates premium and dividend rates, determines what a company's reserve liabilities should be, and establishes nonforfeiture, surrender, and loan values. It also does the research needed to predict mortality and morbidity rates, to establish guidelines for selecting risks, and to determine the profitability of the company's products.

actuarial gains or losses See *experience gains or losses.*

actuarial opinion and memorandum (AOM) An insurer's formal declaration and filing attesting that a valuation actuary has tested the insurer's cash flows under the required scenarios and that the insurer's reserves make adequate provision for the insurer to meet future obligations to customers, considering the assets that are backing the reserves.

actuarial valuation A determination, based on statistical probability by an actuary, of the value of a pension plan's assets and its liabilities to determine if the assets are adequate to fund the plan's liabilities. If the value of the assets is not adequate, the plan sponsor must increase its contributions to make up the deficiency; if the assets are more than adequate, the plan sponsor can reduce contributions. Also called *plan valuation.*

actuary An expert in the mathematics of insurance, annuities, and financial instruments.

AD&D rider See *accidental death and dismemberment (AD&D) rider.*

ADB rider See *accidental death benefit (ADB) rider.*

additional insurance option See *additional term insurance dividend option.*

additional insured rider See *second insured rider.*

additional term insurance dividend option A life insurance policy dividend option under which policy dividends are used as a net single premium to purchase one-year term insurance. Also called the *additional insurance option* or the *fifth dividend option.*

ADEA See *Age Discrimination in Employment Act of 1967 (ADEA).*

adhesion See *contract of adhesion.*

ad hoc adjustments Non-automatic adjustments of a retiree's pension benefits, usually made to reflect the effects of inflation. The adjustments are made through a series of supplemental payments made at intervals determined by the plan sponsor.

adjustable life insurance Life insurance designed to allow the policyowner to alter the amount of the coverage or the amount of the premium as the policyowner's needs change.

adjusted community rating The process of determining a group's premium rate in which an HMO adjusts the standard or pure community rate premium by adding or subtracting an amount that reflects the group's past claims experience. See also *standard community rating.*

adjusted premiums Special premiums, greater than net premiums, that are defined in the Standard Nonforfeiture Law and are used in calculating the legal minimum cash values.

administrative services only (ASO) An arrangement whereby an organization (usually an employer) hires an outside firm to perform specific administrative services, usually including claim administration, for a group benefit program. The organization retains financial responsibility for paying claims. See also *self-insured group insurance* and *third-party administrator (TPA)*.

admitted assets In the United States, those assets that state insurance law permits to be included on the *Assets* page of the Annual Statement.

admitted reinsurer In the United States, a reinsurer that is licensed to accept reinsurance in a given jurisdiction. Also called an *authorized reinsurer*. Contrast with *nonadmitted reinsurer*.

advance and arrears system A premium accounting method used in the home service distribution system. Under this method, the home office charges an agent each month with the amount of all premiums due on the policies that the agent services. When the agent sends the collected premiums to the insurance company, the agent is credited with the amount of premiums collected. See also *home service distribution system* and *industrial insurance*. Contrast with *cash premium accounting system*.

advanced underwriting department An insurance company home office department responsible for providing technical and sales assistance to agents involved in estate planning and business insurance cases. Also known as the *estate planning department*.

advance funding A procedure in which a pension plan sponsor deposits amounts of money in a fund during the working years of plan participants to guarantee payment of pension benefits to the plan participants when they retire.

adverse deviation Actual conditions that differ from an insurer's actuarial assumptions, thus reducing the insurer's revenues, increasing its expenses, or increasing its benefit payments.

adverse selection See *antiselection*.

Age Discrimination in Employment Act of 1967 (ADEA) United States legislation that protects employment rights of individuals age 40 and over. ADEA prohibits age-based firings and generally prevents employers from forcing employees to retire at age 65. In relation to pension plans, ADEA prohibits employers from discontinuing contributions or benefit accruals to an individual's pension plan after that person reaches age 65.

agency See *agency relationship* and *territory.* See also *agency office.*

agency agreement An agreement between a principal and an agent that describes the scope of the agent's actual authority. See *agent* and *principal.*

agency at will An agency relationship that is to continue for an unspecified amount of time. See *agency relationship.*

agency bank A mutual savings bank that does not sell its own savings bank life insurance policies to the public but, instead, sells such policies as an agent for an issuing bank. An agency bank only accepts applications, collects premiums, and provides service for its policyowners. See also *issuing bank* and *savings bank life insurance (SBLI).*

agency by appointment An agency relationship that is created when a principal appoints an agent to act on the principal's behalf. See *agency relationship.* Contrast with *agency by ratification.*

agency by ratification An agency relationship that is created when the principal ratifies a purported agent's unauthorized act. See *agency relationship.* Contrast with *agency by appointment.*

agency office A field office that is established and maintained by a general agent.

agency relationship A legal relationship by which one party, the agent, is authorized to perform certain acts on behalf of the other party, the principal.

agency system   A distribution system in which insurance companies use their own commissioned agents to sell and deliver insurance policies. The agency system is the most common system for distributing individual life insurance products and includes the branch office distribution system and the general agency distribution system. Also called the *ordinary agency system.* See also *branch office distribution system, brokerage distribution system,* and *general agency distribution system.*

agency underwriting manual   An abridged edition of an insurer's home office underwriting manual that usually presents an abbreviated list of impairments and possible underwriting actions. See also *underwriting manual.*

agent   A party who is authorized by another party, the principal, to act on the principal's behalf in contractual dealings with third parties. Called a *mandatary* in Quebec. See also *insurance agent.*

agent of record   The agent or broker who is recognized by the insurer as the person to whom the commission is to be paid.

agent-owned reinsurance company (AORC)   A captive reinsurance company formed by an insurance company and owned by a group of the company's agents. The company insures all business written by those agents with the captive so that the agents can share in the profits of their own labor.

agent's lien   An agent's right to satisfy his or her lawful claims against the principal from any of the principal's property that is in the agent's possession. See *agent* and *principal.*

agent's statement   The portion of the insurance application in which the agent reports anything he or she knows or suspects about the proposed insured that is not reported by the applicant or proposed insured.

age of majority   The age at which a person has the legal capacity to enter into and be bound by a contract.

aggregate claims   In health insurance, the claim frequency rate per insured multiplied by the average amount of each claim and then multiplied by the number of insured lives. The aggregate claims expected under the terms of a health insurance contract are a primary element in calculating health insurance premium rates.

aggregate funding methods   Pension plan funding methods in which the amount of contributions necessary to fund a plan is determined in the aggregate for all plan participants, rather than separately for each individual plan participant. Contrast with *individual funding methods.*

aggregate mortality table   A mortality table based on the experience of all insured lives, including mortality rates both during and after the select period. The mortality rates of an aggregate mortality table fall between those of a select mortality table and those of an ultimate mortality table. See also *mortality table, select mortality table, select period,* and *ultimate mortality table.*

aggregate stop-loss coverage   A type of stop-loss insurance that provides benefits when the group's total claims exceed a stated amount within a stated period of time. See also *stop-loss insurance* and *individual stop-loss coverage.*

AIME   See *average indexed monthly earnings (AIME).*

aleatory contract   A contract under which one party provides something of value to another party in exchange for a conditional promise, which is a promise that the other party will perform a stated act if a specified, uncertain event occurs. Insurance contracts are aleatory because the policyowner pays premiums to the insurer, and in return the insurer promises to pay benefits if the event insured against occurs.

alien insurer   In the United States, an insurer that is incorporated under the laws of another country. Compare to *domestic insurer* and *foreign insurer.*

alienation of benefits In pension planning, the assignment of a plan participant's benefits to an individual other than the participant. In the United States, ERISA generally prohibits the alienation of benefits, although exceptions to this rule include the use of a participant's vested benefit as collateral for a loan. The ERISA prohibition on alienation of benefits prevents creditors from attaching an individual's pension benefits.

all-causes deductible In health insurance, a deductible which need only be satisfied once during a given period of time. If the period of time is a calendar year, as it usually is, then this type of deductible is known as a calendar year deductible. Contrast with *per-cause deductible.*

all-lines exclusive agency system See *multiple-line agency (MLA) system.*

allocated funding A method of funding a pension plan in which a portion of the total plan funds is allocated to each participant. This type of funding is often achieved through the purchase of annuities or insurance contracts for each participant. Contrast with *unallocated funding.*

allowable expenses Reasonable and customary medical expenses incurred by an insured and covered under at least one of the insured's group medical expense plans; under a COB provision, the total amount of benefits that the insured is eligible to receive from all of his medical expense plans.

allowance In reinsurance, an amount paid by the reinsurer to the ceding company to help cover the ceding company's acquisition and other costs and sometimes to provide some profit to the ceding company. Also called a *ceding commission.*

alphabet split In an automatic reinsurance treaty, a method of allocating policies between two or more reinsurers by assigning each reinsurer a certain portion of the alphabet, for example A through K or L through Z, and reinsuring each policy with the appropriate reinsurer according to the insured's name.

Amendments to the Standard Valuation Law The NAIC's official 1980 revisions to the older Standard Valuation Law. The original Standard Valuation Law and the amendments set forth criteria for setting nonforfeiture values and policy reserves. See also *Standard Valuation Law.*

American Council of Life Insurance (ACLI) In the United States, an organization which collects and disseminates data on life insurance markets.

American rule A general rule of law stating that, if several assignees notify an insurer of the assignment of a life insurance or annuity policy, the assignee with priority to the policy proceeds is the assignee to whom the first assignment was made. See also *English rule.*

anniversary See *policy anniversary.*

annual claim costs Used in calculating net annual premiums for health insurance. Annual claim costs are equal to the expected number of claims for one year multiplied by the average amount payable for each claim. Annual claim costs are calculated for each age and sex and, if appropriate, for each occupational class and geographical region.

Annual Information Return In Canada, a report containing financial and other information that pension plans must file annually with the appropriate provincial or federal government.

Annual Report Form 5500 In the United States, a detailed report of membership and financial information pertaining to the operation of a pension plan. This report must be filed annually with the Internal Revenue Service.

Annual Return An accounting form filed in each province in which an insurer conducts business and with the federal Office of the Superintendent of Financial Institutions by every insurer subject to federal regulation in Canada.

Annual Statement   An accounting report prepared by each insurer every year and filed with the National Association of Insurance Commission (NAIC) and the insurance department in each state in which the insurer operates. This report contains detailed accounting and statistical data that regulators use to evaluate a life and health insurance company's solvency and its compliance with insurance laws.

annually renewable term (ART) insurance   See *yearly renewable term (YRT) insurance.*

annuitant   The person whose lifetime is used as the measuring period to determine how long benefits are payable under a life annuity. In many cases, an annuity's *contractowner, payee,* and *annuitant* may be the same person.

annuity   (1) A series of payments made or received at regular intervals. (2) A policy under which an insurance company promises to make a series of periodic payments to a named individual in exchange for a premium or a series of premiums. There are many kinds of annuities. For the annuities identified in this glossary, see *annuity certain, annuity due, annuity immediate, deferred annuity, deferred life annuity, disabled life annuity, flexible premium annuity, group deferred annuity, immediate annuity, joint and survivor annuity, level premium annuity, life annuity, life annuity with period certain, refund annuity, single premium annuity, single premium deferred annuity (SPDA), straight life annuity, temporary life annuity, variable annuity, and whole life annuity.*

annuity beneficiary   The individual the contractowner names to receive any survivor benefits payable during the accumulation period of a deferred annuity.

annuity certain   An annuity that provides a benefit amount payable for a specified period of time regardless of whether any individual lives or dies.

annuity due   A series of payments in which the payments are made at the beginning of each payment period. Contrast with *immediate annuity.*

annuity factor   The present value at age *x* of a temporary life annuity of 1.

annuity immediate   A series of payments in which the payments are made at the end of each payment period. Also called *ordinary annuity.* Contrast with *annuity due.*

annuity mortality table   Table listing the projected mortality rates for persons purchasing annuities. Used by actuaries to calculate premiums and reserves for annuities in which benefits are paid only if a designated person is alive. Annuity mortality tables usually project lower rates of mortality than do mortality tables that are used for life insurance. See also *mortality table.*

annuity period   The time between each of the payments in the series of periodic annuity benefit payments.

annuity units   The term used for ownership shares in a variable annuity's separate-account fund after the accumulation period has ended. Annuity units are bought with accumulation units and are used to determine benefit payment amounts. See also *accumulation units.*

antiselection   The tendency of people who believe they have a greater-than-average likelihood of loss to apply for or continue insurance to a greater extent than do other people. Also called *adverse selection* or *selection against the insurer.*

AOM   See *actuarial opinion and memorandum (AOM).*

AORC   See *agent-owned reinsurance company (AORC).*

APL   See *automatic premium loan (APL).*

apparent authority   Authority that is not expressly conferred on an agent but that the principal either intentionally or negligently allows a third party to believe the agent possesses. See *agent* and *principal.* Compare to *express authority* and *implied authority.*

applicant   The party applying for an insurance policy.

application   A form that must be completed by an individual or other party who is seeking insurance coverage. This form provides the insurance company with much of the information it will need to decide whether to accept or reject the risk.

appropriated surplus   See *special surplus fund.*

approval type temporary insurance agreement   An agreement issued in conjunction with a conditional premium receipt that provides temporary life insurance coverage as of the date the insurer approves the proposed insured as a standard risk. See also *conditional premium receipt* and *temporary insurance agreements*. Compare to *insurability type temporary insurance agreement.*

APS   See *Attending Physician's Statement (APS).*

ART   See *yearly renewable term insurance (YRT).*

ASO   See *administrative services only (ASO).*

assessment method   An early method for funding life insurance in which the estimated annual cost of paying death benefits was shared equally by participants in the insurance plan. Also called the *pre-death assessment method*. See also *mutual benefit method.*

asset-liability management   A program that coordinates the administration of an insurer's investments with the administration of its policy liabilities.

assets   All things of value owned by an individual or organization.

asset share   The net amount of cash per unit of coverage—often per $1,000 of face value in force—that an insurance or annuity product has accumulated at a given time.

asset-share model A mathematical simulation model used by insurance companies to indicate how a product's assets can be expected to grow and when the product can be expected to become profitable.

asset valuation reserve (AVR) Under statutory accounting in the United States, an Annual Statement account that absorbs an insurer's credit-related gains and losses on its investments and minimizes the effects of those gains and losses on the insurer's capital and surplus.

assigned surplus See *special surplus fund.*

assignee The party to whom all or certain contractual rights are transferred under an absolute or collateral assignment.

assignment An agreement under which one party—the assignor—transfers some or all of his ownership rights in a particular property to another party—the assignee. See also *absolute assignment* and *collateral assignment.*

assignment of benefits An authorization directing an insurer to make payment directly to a provider of benefits, such as a physician or dentist, rather than to the insured.

assignment provision A life insurance policy provision that describes the roles of the insurer and the policyowner when the policy is assigned.

assignor The owner of property who transfers certain rights in that property to another party by means of an absolute or collateral assignment.

association group insurance Group insurance extended to the members of a trade, professional, or other association.

assuming company In a reinsurance transaction, the insurer that accepts risk on a contract issued by another insurance company.

assumption The acceptance of risk in an insurance or a reinsurance transaction.

assumption certificate In an assumption reinsurance agreement, a new insurance certificate issued on an existing insurance contract. The certificate indicates a reinsurer has assumed from the ceding company all of the risk under the contract.

assumption reinsurance A reinsurance agreement by which one company permanently transfers full responsibility for a block of policies to another company. After the cession, the ceding company is no longer a party to the insurance agreement.

assumptions See *actuarial assumptions.*

attachment point The retention limit specified in an excess-of-loss reinsurance agreement.

attained age The current age of an insured.

attained age conversion The conversion of a life insurance policy from one form of insurance to another (such as from term life insurance to whole life insurance) at a premium rate that is based on the age of the insured person at the time of the conversion.

Attending Physician's Statement (APS) A written statement from a physician who has treated, or is currently treating, a proposed insured or an insured for one or more conditions. The statement provides the insurance company with information relevant to underwriting a risk or settling a claim.

attorney in fact A layperson acting with a claimant's power of attorney regarding a claim.

authorized reinsurer See *admitted reinsurer.*

automatic binding authority See *automatic binding limit.*

automatic binding limit Under an automatic reinsurance treaty, the dollar amount of risk a reinsurer will obligate itself to accept without making its own underwriting assessment of the risk. Also called the *binding limit* or the *automatic binding authority.*

automatic dividend option For a particular life insurance policy, the dividend option that applies if the policyowner does not choose an option. The most common automatic dividend option is the *paid-up additional insurance dividend option.* See *dividend options.*

automatic nonforfeiture option For a particular life insurance policy, a specified nonforfeiture benefit that becomes effective automatically when a renewal premium is not paid by the end of the grace period and the policyowner has not elected another nonforfeiture option. The most common automatic nonforfeiture option is the *extended term insurance option.* See also *nonforfeiture options.*

automatic premium loan (APL) A life insurance policy provision that allows the insurer to pay an overdue premium on a policy by making a loan against the policy's cash value.

automatic reinsurance treaty A reinsurance agreement in which the reinsurer agrees, for a stipulated type of risk, to accept each risk or a portion of each risk submitted by the ceding company, up to a certain limit, provided the ceding company insures up to its usual retention limit. In this agreement, the ceding company assumes full underwriting responsibility for all cases reinsured.

average indexed monthly earnings (AIME) In the United States, the figure on which social security disability, retirement and other benefits are based. The figure is an average of the monthly earnings on which a worker has paid social security tax. The figure is indexed, that is, adjusted to compensate for inflation.

average premium For a group insurance contract, the amount of premium usually charged for a specific amount of insurance. For example, the average premium rate for a group life insurance contract is often a certain amount per $1,000 of insurance. Sometimes called *final premium.*

aviation exclusion A life insurance contract provision which specifies that the death benefit is not payable if the insured dies because of certain aviation activities.

AVR See *asset valuation reserve (AVR)*.

baby group plan See *small group insurance plan*.

back-dating Making the effective date of an insurance policy earlier than the date of the application so that the premium rate will be lower. State law usually limits back-dating to not more than six months. Also called *dating back*.

back-loaded policy A life insurance policy (usually a universal life insurance policy) in which most of the expense charges occur when the policyowner surrenders the policy or makes cash withdrawals from the policy. Such charges are usually highest in the early policy years and are often eliminated at the end of a certain number of years. See also *front-loaded policy* and *universal life insurance*.

backloading The practice of providing a higher accrual of pension benefits during a participant's later years of employment. The practice is designed to encourage and reward long service.

banding A pricing system for bundled products under which an insurer establishes several premium rate ranges (bands) according to the face amount of a policy. The premium rate per $1,000 decreases as the face amount increases.

basic death benefit The death benefit according to the terms of the original, basic contract of a life insurance policy. The basic death benefit does not include the benefit for any supplementary riders, such as an accidental death benefit (ADB) rider. For policies in which the death benefit remains constant, the basic death benefit is equivalent to the face amount. Compare to *death benefit* and *policy proceeds*.

basic experience table See *basic mortality table*.

basic medical expense coverage Health insurance coverage that consists of separate benefits for each specific type of covered medical care cost, including hospital expense coverage, surgical expense coverage, and physicians' expense coverage.

basic mortality table A mortality table with no safety margin built into the mortality rates. Also called a *basic experience table.* See also *mortality table* and *safety margin.*

basic services Under dental insurance, dental services, such as fillings, periodontics, and oral surgery, which are often covered at 80 percent of their reasonable and customary charges.

basket clause (1) From an investment point of view, a provision that allows insurance companies to invest a small percentage of their assets generally without regard to statutory restrictions. (2) From an accounting point of view, a clause that permits life and health insurers to hold a specified amount of their assets as nonauthorized assets, which are not restricted in the same way as authorized assets.

beneficiary The person or party the owner of an insurance policy names to receive the policy benefit if the event insured against occurs. See also *contingent beneficiary, irrevocable beneficiary, primary beneficiary,* and *revocable beneficiary.*

beneficiary declaration In Canada, an insurance policy beneficiary designation that is made in a separate written document after the insurance policy has been issued.

beneficiary for value Under prior Canadian insurance law, a person named as a life insurance policy beneficiary in return for providing valuable consideration to the policyowner. The 1962 revision of the Uniform Life Insurance Act abolished this class of beneficiaries.

benefit The amount of money paid when an insurance claim is approved. Also called the *policy benefit.*

benefit of survivorship The concept that annuity payments will be made as long as the designated recipient is alive at the time the payment is due. This concept is used in the calculation of amounts due under life insurance settlement options.

benefit period The time during which periodic income benefits will be paid under a disability income insurance policy.

benefits budget A type of expense budget indicating the amount of money a company expects to pay for claims, cash surrenders, and policy dividends during the next year.

benefit schedule Under a group insurance plan, a table or schedule that specifies the amount of coverage provided for each class of insured. Insureds are often classified with reference either to earnings or to rank or position. Also known as *schedule of benefits.*

best-earnings plan A pension plan which specifies that each participant's benefit will be calculated according to the final-average formula.

bill of interpleader See *interpleader.*

binding limit See *automatic binding limit.*

binding premium receipt A type of premium receipt that provides a potential insured with temporary insurance coverage from the time the applicant receives the receipt until the insurer declines the application or issues and delivers a policy. Compare to *conditional premium receipt.*

birthday rule According to some coordination of benefits provisions, the method used to define which plan is the primary payor for an individual who is covered as a dependent under more than one group health insurance plan. According to the birthday rule, the plan covering the employee whose birth date falls earlier in the calendar year is the primary payor for the dependent. Also known as the *earlier birthday method.*

blended rating A method of setting group insurance premium rates under which the insurer uses a blend of experience rating and manual rating. Blended rates are used to determine the appropriate group insurance premium rates for intermediate-size groups. See also *experience rating* and *manual rating.*

Blue Cross plan A hospital expense insurance plan offered by a regionally-operated health care provider affiliated with a large national non-profit health care organization.

Blue Shield plan A physician expense insurance plan offered by a regionally-operated health care provider affiliated with a large national nonprofit health care organization.

bonus additions In Canada, paid-up additional insurance or one-year term insurance purchased with policy dividends.

bordereau In a reinsurance arrangement, a report provided regularly by the ceding company to the reinsurer containing information about the reinsured risks. A bordereau frequently includes information about insureds, the details of their coverage, and their premium status. Bordereaux are used in self-administered reinsurance arrangements in lieu of cession cards. See *cession card* and *self-administration.*

branch manager The individual in charge of a branch office. A branch manager is an employee of the insurance company. Also called a *general manager.*

branch office A field office that is established and maintained by an insurance company.

break-even period See *validation period.*

break-even point See *validation point.*

break in service The length of time between the date an employee leaves a firm and the date the employee resumes working for that firm. For pension and employee benefit plan purposes in the United States, a plan participant cannot be deprived of benefits which accumulate before a break in service unless the break is longer than (1) five years or (2) the amount of time that the participant has been employed when the break commences, whichever is greater.

bridging benefit See *bridging supplement.*

bridging supplement In Canada, a supplemental pension provided to a pension plan participant who retires before age 65. The bridging supplement is generally used to integrate private pension plans with public pension plans. If a pension plan participant retires before age 65, the plan sponsor can provide a bridging supplement until the retiree begins to receive payments from the public pension plans at age 65. The combined benefit payment that the participant receives remains level and is the same as the participant would have received had he or she waited until reaching age 65 before beginning to receive benefits. The sponsor is providing an amount *in addition to* the basic pension payment. Also known as a *bridging benefit.* Compare to the *notched option.*

British insurer In Canada, an insurance company incorporated under the laws of either the United Kingdom or any British Commonwealth country besides Canada.

broker (1) A commissioned sales agent who is under contract to and sells the insurance products of more than one insurance company. (2) For a career agent, to submit insurance applications to companies other than the agent's own company.

brokerage distribution system A distribution system that relies on commissioned agents, called brokers, who sell the products of more than one insurance company.

brokerage general agency See *brokerage shop.*

brokerage manager A salaried insurance company employee or an independent agent whose responsibility is to appoint brokers on behalf of the company and to encourage brokers to sell the products of a particular insurance company.

brokerage shop An agency operated by an independent general agent who is under contract to a number of insurance companies. Also known as a *brokerage general agency.*

broker-dealer A firm that provides information or advice to its customers regarding the sale and/or purchase of securities and that serves as a financial intermediary between buyers and sellers by manufacturing or acquiring securities in order to market them to its customers.

bundled insurance product An insurance product in which the mortality, investment, and expense factors used to calculate premium rates and cash values are not identified separately in the policy. Traditional whole life insurance is an example of a bundled insurance product. See also *unbundled insurance product.*

business-continuation insurance An insurance plan that enables the owner(s) of a business to provide for the continued operation of the business if the owner or a key person dies. See *cross-purchase method, entity method,* and *key-person life insurance.*

business insurance Insurance that is intended to serve the insurance needs of a business rather than the needs of an individual.

Buyer's Guide In the United States, a publication that many states require insurance companies to give to an applicant for life insurance. The Buyer's Guide helps the applicant make an informed choice among policies.

buy-out See *financial settlement.*

buy-sell agreement An agreement in which one party agrees to purchase a second party's financial interest in a business following the second party's death and the second party agrees to direct her estate to sell that interest to the purchasing party. The purchase is often financed with the proceeds of a life insurance policy.

cafeteria plan An employee benefit plan that gives each employee several choices as to the types and/or amounts of group benefits. Also known as a *flexible benefit plan.*

calendar year deductible In health insurance, a deductible that need only be satisfied once during a calendar year.

Canada Pension Plan (CPP) In Canada, a federal program that provides a pension for Canadian wage earners who have contributed money into the plan during their working years. The plan also provides some other benefits, including long-term disability income benefits. The plan covers workers in all provinces except Quebec. See also *Quebec Pension Plan (QPP)*.

Canadian Council of Insurance Regulators (CCIR) A Canadian organization of provincial insurance regulators whose purpose is to discuss insurance issues and to develop model insurance legislation that it encourages provincial legislatures to adopt. Similar to the National Association of Insurance Commissioners in the United States.

Canadian Institute of Chartered Accountants (CICA) Handbook Section 3460 See *Section 3460.*

Canadian Life and Health Insurance Association (CLHIA) An association comprised of most of the life and health insurance companies in Canada. The CLHIA conducts research on insurance issues and promotes the best interests of the industry. It is the primary source of information about the life and health insurance industy in Canada.

Canadian Life and Health Insurance Compensation Corporation (CompCorp) In Canada, a federally incorporated, nonprofit company established by the Canadian Life and Health Insurance Association (CLHIA) to guarantee payment of benefits, up to specified limits, under covered policies of an insolvent member company.

Canadian Reinsurance Conference A Canadian group which meets annually to discuss subjects of importance to companies involved in reinsurance, such as standards of conduct in the reinsurance industry.

Canadian Reinsurance Guidelines A set of guidelines developed by the Canadian Reinsurance Conference to standardize reinsurance procedures. Although the guidelines do not have any formal authority, they are generally accepted as representing standard industry practice in Canada.

cancellable policy   An individual health insurance policy that grants the insurer the right to terminate the policy at any time, for any reason. See also *conditionally renewable policy, guaranteed renewable policy, noncancellable and guaranteed renewable policy, noncancellable policy,* and *optionally renewable policy.*

canned presentations   See *sales tracks.*

capacity   The largest amount of insurance an insurer or a reinsurer is willing or able to underwrite. The term can refer to an insurer's capacity on one individual or to the insurer's capacity for all its business.

capital and surplus ratios   A method by which insurance companies measure their financial strength by comparing their capital and surplus to their liabilities, often taking into account other factors. See also *Minimum Continuing Capital and Surplus Requirements (MCCSR)* and *Risk-Based Capital (RBC) requirements.*

capitation   A compensation plan used in some health maintenance organizations (HMOs) in which a physician is paid a flat amount—usually on a monthly basis—for each subscriber who has elected to use that physician. See also *fee schedule payment structure.*

captive agents   See *exclusive agents.*

captive insurance company   An insurance company, formed and controlled by a separate company, that provides insurance to the controlling company. Companies that form captive insurance companies include all types of companies that extend credit to customers, including banks and retailers. See also *agent-owned reinsurance company (AORC).*

career agent   A full-time commissioned salesperson who works out of an insurance company's field office, holds an agent contract with that company, and sends all, or almost all, of his or her business to that company. A career agent may occasionally broker business with other companies.

career average (career earnings) benefit formula A type of defined benefit formula in which the retirement benefit amount is derived on the basis of a participant's compensation during the entire period of participation in the plan. See also *defined benefit formula*. Contrast with *final average (final earnings) benefit formula.*

Career Profile System A system developed by the Life Insurance Marketing and Research Association (LIMRA) that gathers information about a job candidate's work history and personal background so that insurance agencies can try to predict the candidate's likelihood for success as an insurance agent or a financial services consultant.

carry-over provision A provision found in most medical expense policies stating that expenses incurred during the last three months of a benefit period that are used to satisfy the current benefit period's deductible may be used to satisfy any or all of the following benefit period's deductible.

case management A utilization management technique that addresses the medical necessity of care as well as alternative treatments or solutions, especially when the patient is likely to require very expensive treatment. Also known as *catastrophic claim management, large claim management,* or *medical case management.* See also *utilization management.*

cash-balance pension plan A type of defined benefit plan in which each participant has an account that is credited with amounts reflecting the employer's contributions and amounts reflecting investment interest. The balance in the account indicates the participant's accrued benefit. Upon retirement or withdrawal, the participant may receive the full account balance in a lump sum, provided that the benefits are fully vested, or may use the account balance to purchase an annuity.

cash dividend See *dividend.*

cash dividend option See *cash payment option.*

cash-flow testing An analysis that involves forecasting, under a number of different scenarios, the timing and amount of the revenues and expenses relative to some or all of an insurer's business.

Cash or Deferred Arrangement (CODA) See *Section 401(k) plan.*

cash payment option A life insurance policy dividend option under which policy dividends are paid to the policyowner in cash.

cash premium accounting system A system in which a home service agent personally collects premium payments from each policyowner and records each transaction in a route collection book or computer. The agent then remits the premiums to the home office, which updates the policy records to reflect these collections and prepares new route collection records. Contrast with *advance and arrears system.*

cash refund annuity A refund annuity under which the refund is paid in a lump sum.

cash refund option A form of the *life income option with refund* which specifies that any proceeds remaining when the beneficiary dies will be paid in a lump sum to the contingent payee. Contrast with the *installment refund option.*

cash surrender value (1) In a life insurance policy, the amount of money, adjusted for factors such as policy loans or late premiums, that the policyowner will receive if the policyowner cancels the coverage and surrenders the policy to the insurance company. Also called the *net cash value.* Compare to *cash value.* (2) In an annuity, the amount that a contractowner will receive if he surrenders a deferred annuity. This amount is equal to the accumulated value of the annuity less any surrender charges specified in the policy.

cash surrender value nonforfeiture option A life insurance policy nonforfeiture option which specifies that a policyowner who discontinues premium payments can elect to surrender the policy and receive the policy's cash surrender value.

cash value In a life insurance policy, the amount of money, before adjustment for factors such as policy loans or late premiums, that the policyowner will receive if the policyowner allows the policy to lapse or cancels the coverage and surrenders the policy to the insurance company. Cash values are a feature of most types of permanent life insurance, such as whole life and universal life. Compare to *cash surrender value.* Also called *inside build-up* and *policyowner's equity.*

catastrophic claim management See *case management.*

catastrophic reinsurance plan A reinsurance plan which specifies that, when a certain minimum number of claims result from a single accidental occurrence, such as more than two claims resulting from an airplane crash, a hurricane, or an earthquake, the reinsurer pays losses in excess of the plan deductible. The reinsurer's liability is limited to a maximum amount per catastrophe. Sometimes called *catastrophe reinsurance* or *cat cover.*

cat cover See *catastrophic reinsurance plan.*

causal relation requirements Proof required by statute in Kansas, Missouri, Rhode Island, and Puerto Rico to show that the facts misrepresented in an application for insurance were related to the loss insured against.

CCIR See *Canadian Council of Insurance Regulators (CCIR).*

cede To obtain reinsurance on insurance policies by transferring all or part of the risk to a reinsurer.

ceding commission See *allowance.*

ceding company In a reinsurance transaction, the insurer that purchases reinsurance to cover all or part of those risks that it does not wish to retain in full. Also called the *direct insurer, direct writer,* or *direct-writing company.*

center of influence A person who has many contacts in a community and who is willing to refer or recommend an agent to those people.

certain payment A payment that, not being contingent upon any predesignated condition, will definitely be made under any circumstances.

certificate holder A member of an insured group who has received a certificate of insurance.

certificate of assumption In assumption reinsurance, a certificate sent to each policyholder whose policy has been ceded to give the policyowner (1) notice of the assumption and (2) information concerning the new insurer.

certificate of authority (1) A document created by an insurer detailing the authority granted to an agent or group of agents to act on behalf of the insurer. (2) In the United States, a certificate issued by a state's insurance department authorizing an insurer to issue certain types of insurance within the state.

certificate of coverage (COC) A plan booklet that describes the benefits, features, and services of an HMO's plan.

certificate of indebtedness A certificate issued by an insurer to the beneficiary of a life insurance policy that specifies a guaranteed minimum interest rate and the frequency with which the insurer will make interest payments under the interest settlement option.

certificate of insurance A document that describes the coverage provided by a group insurance policy and that is distributed by the group policyholder to each group insured. See also *master contract.*

cession (1) In reinsurance, the act of ceding. (2) In reinsurance, a parcel or unit of insurance that a company cedes to a reinsurer. Called *guarantee* in Canada.

cession card In a reinsurance relationship which is not self-administered, a card used by the ceding company and the reinsurer in their communications with each other to indicate the cession of a risk. See also *individual cession administration.*

change of condition provision An insurance provision stipulating that, for a policy to become effective, all conditions described in the application must still be true at the time of delivery.

change of occupation provision An individual health insurance policy provision that grants the insurer the right to adjust a policy's premium rate or benefits when the insured changes to a more or less hazardous occupation.

children's insurance rider A rider that may be added to a permanent life insurance policy to provide term insurance coverage on the insured's children.

claim A request for payment under the terms of an insurance policy.

claim administration department The department in a life and health insurance company responsible for processing claims. In this department, claim examiners review claims presented by policyowners or beneficiaries, verify the validity of claims, and authorize the payment of benefits to the proper person.

claim analyst See *claim examiner.*

claimant The person or party making a formal request for payment of benefits due under the terms of an insurance contract.

claim approver See *claim examiner.*

claim costs The costs an insurer incurs to provide the policy benefits it has promised. Insurers calculate expected claim costs in order to calculate net premium rates.

claim examiner   An employee of an insurance company whose responsibilities include investigating claims, approving the claims that are valid, and denying those that are invalid or fraudulent. Also called *claim analyst, claim approver,* or *claim specialist.*

claim fluctuation reserve   Usually associated with small group insurance policies, a claim fluctuation reserve is a fund established by an insurer and designed to protect the insurer against unfavorable claims experience. By setting aside funds in such a reserve, the insurance company can offer a small group relatively stable premium rates in future years. For a listing of other types of reserves, see *reserve.*

claim frequency rate   In health insurance calculations, the claim frequency rate is the expected percentage of insured people who will file claims and the number of claims they will file during a given period. The claim frequency rate is used to calculate average claim costs, which are used to calculate premium rates.

claim investigation   The process of obtaining necessary claim information in order to decide whether or not to pay a claim.

claim reserve   A liability account reflecting the present value of amounts that an insurer will pay in the future on claims that have been reported but which the insurer has not yet paid in full. See also *disabled life reserve.*

claim specialist   See *claim examiner.*

class beneficiary designation   A beneficiary designation that names several people as a group—for example, "children of the insured"—rather than naming each person individually.

class of policies   All policies of a particular type that an insurer has issued, or all policies an insurer has issued to a particular group of insureds.

clean-up fund   A lump-sum life insurance death benefit designed to pay the insured's outstanding debts and final expenses.

CLHIA See *Canadian Life and Health Insurance Association (CLHIA).*

CLHIA Guidelines Recommended guidelines insurers are expected to abide by as a condition of membership in the Canadian Life and Health Insurance Association (CLHIA).

client and policy master file The data base that provides much of the information about individuals and individual policies for an insurer's management information system.

client service department See *customer service department.*

closed contract An insurance contract in which the terms of the insurance contract and the application constitute the entire agreement between the policyowner and the insurer. Commercial insurance companies use closed contracts. See also *open contract.*

closed-panel HMO A type of HMO that requires physicians either to belong to a special group of physicians that has contracted with the HMO or to be employees of the HMO in order to provide services to HMO members.

closing The process of securing a purchase commitment from a prospect by requesting and obtaining the prospect's agreement to submit an application for the coverage recommended in a sales proposal.

COB clause See *coordination of benefits (COB) clause.*

COBRA See *Consolidated Omnibus Budget Reconciliation Act of 1985 (COBRA).*

COC See *certificate of coverage (COC).*

CODA See *Section 401(k) plan.*

coinsurance (1) In a health insurance policy, the percentage of all eligible medical expenses, in excess of the deductible, that an insured is required to pay. Also called *percentage participation.* (2) A type of reinsurance plan in which the ceding company pays the reinsurer part of the premium paid by the insured, minus a proportionate share of the commission and premium taxes associated with the policy that is being reinsured and a portion of the ceding company's general overhead expenses. In return, the reinsurer agrees to pay the ceding company a proportionate part of the death benefit when a claim is filed and to contribute to all other policy benefits, including dividends, on a scale determined by the ceding company. In addition, the reinsurer agrees to accumulate the required reserves for the reinsured portion of the policy.

coinsurance provision   An expense participation feature included in many medical expense insurance policies. The provision requires the insured to pay a specified percentage of all covered medical expenses remaining after the policy's deductible has been met.

COLA   See *cost-of-living adjustment (COLA)*.

cold calling   A prospecting method in which a sales agent calls or visits prospects with whom he has had no prior contact.

collateral assignment   A transfer of some ownership rights in a contract from one party to another, generally for a temporary period. Insurance policies are often assigned as collateral for a loan, in which case all transferred rights revert to the assignor when the loan is repaid. See also *assignment*.

collected premiums   The amount of premium income received by an insurance company during an accounting period.

collection report   A weekly or monthly report, prepared by a home service insurance agent, that shows the total premiums collected, the premiums paid in advance, and the premiums overdue.

combination company   A life and health insurance company that sells both industrial and ordinary insurance products.

combination clause A clause in a disability income contract that specifies a point at which the definition of total disability will no longer be based on an insured's inability to perform his or her "own occupation" but on the insured's inability to perform "any occupation."

combination dental plan A dental plan that contains features of both scheduled and nonscheduled plans. Typically, combination plans cover preventive and diagnostic procedures on a nonscheduled basis and other services on a scheduled basis. See also *nonscheduled dental plan* and *scheduled dental plan.*

combination plan A pension plan that employs an approach to funding wherein part of the funding is allocated and part is unallocated. The allocated part of the employer's contribution is used to purchase annuities or life insurance contracts with cash values. The unallocated part is placed in a side fund, also called a conversion fund. See also *allocated funding* and *unallocated funding.*

combined ratio In health insurance, a calculation that indicates whether the premiums being collected are sufficient to pay both policyowners' claims and the company's expenses; the sum of the loss ratio and the expense ratio.

commingling of funds The illegal misuse of funds by combining monies belonging to policyowners with an agent's own funds.

commission The amount of money paid to an insurance agent for selling an insurance policy. A commission is almost always calculated as a percentage of the premium.

commission chargeback A charge against an agent's commission account to repay the company for all or part of a commission previously credited to the agent. Commission chargebacks are made on an agent's account, for example, when premiums are returned to the policyowner or when a policy for which an agent receives an annualized commission lapses before the end of the policy year.

Commissioners Reserve Valuation Method (CRVM) A method prescribed in the United States for calculating modified net premiums and reserves for life insurance policies.

common accident provision (1) A provision, included in many medical expense insurance contracts, that specifies if two or more members of the same family are injured in the same accident, their combined medical expenses will only be subject to one deductible. (2) A provision, found in many voluntary group accidental death and dismemberment plans, which specifies that the amount payable by the insurance company is limited to a stipulated maximum for all employees killed or injured in a single accident.

common disaster clause A life insurance policy provision which states that the primary beneficiary must survive the insured by a specified period, such as 60 or 90 days, in order to receive the policy proceeds. Otherwise, the policy proceeds will be paid as though the primary beneficiary had died before the insured. Also known as a *delay clause, survivorship clause,* or *time clause.*

community rating See *adjusted community rating, community rating by class, pooling,* and *standard community rating.*

community rating by class The process of determining HMO premium rates in which the HMO categorizes its members into classes based on age, gender, marital status, or some other demographic variable, and charges the same premium to all members of the same class.

commutation See *financial settlement.*

commutation function A quantity representing a combination of mortality table figures and interest table figures used to simplify calculations of annuities, premiums, and reserves.

commuted commissions The present value of future renewal commissions. Commuted commissions are sometimes paid instead of renewal commissions.

commuted value In Canada, the present value of the pension benefits expected to be paid to a retiree from the date of retirement until death.

company retention method A method of comparing the costs of various life insurance policies wherein the present value of premiums, cash values, and dividends is calculated by weighting each item each year by the probability that it will be paid. See also *cost comparison methods.*

CompCorp See *Canadian Life and Health Insurance Compensation Corporation (CompCorp).*

comprehensive major medical insurance Medical expense insurance that covers, under one policy, most of the medical expenses an insured may incur, including hospital expenses, surgical expenses, physician expenses, and often other medical expenses.

concurrent review A component of utilization review under which the utilization review organization monitors an insured's treatment and prognosis while he is in the hospital.

conditional premium receipt A type of premium receipt that specifies certain conditions that must be met before temporary life insurance coverage will become effective. See *premium receipt.* Also called a *conditional receipt.* Compare to *binding premium receipt.* See also *approval type temporary insurance agreement* and *insurability type temporary insurance agreement.*

conditionally renewable policy An individual health insurance policy that grants the insurer a limited right to refuse to renew the policy at the end of a premium payment period. The insurer also may increase the premium rate for any class of conditionally renewable policies. See also *cancellable policy, guaranteed renewable policy, noncancellable and guaranteed renewable policy, noncancellable policy,* and *optionally renewable policy.*

conditionally vested commission A commission that begins as a nonvested commission and becomes vested—guaranteed payable to an agent—after the agent attains a certain age or number of years of service. Also known as an *earned commission.*

confirmation certificate A certificate issued to the beneficiary of a life insurance policy that outlines the amount of life insurance proceeds in a retained asset account, the account number, and the current interest rate.

conservation An agent's or an insurer's efforts to prevent a policy from lapsing.

conservative mortality table A mortality table containing mortality rates that are higher than expected if used for life insurance calculations or lower than expected if used for annuity calculations. See also *mortality table.*

Consolidated Omnibus Budget Reconciliation Act of 1985 (COBRA) In the United States, a statute which requires that employers sponsoring group health plans offer continuation of coverage under the group plan to employees and their spouses and dependent children who have lost coverage because of the occurrence of a "qualifying event." Qualifying events include reduction in work hours, many types of termination of employment, death, and divorce.

constructive delivery Legally equivalent to physical delivery of a policy. Constructive delivery occurs (a) when an insurer parts with control of the policy with the intention that the insurer will be uncondition-ally bound by the policy as a completed instrument or (b) when the policy is physically delivered to an agent of the applicant.

consumer report As defined by the Fair Credit Reporting Act, a consumer reporting agency's communication of any information pertaining to an individual consumer's creditworthiness, credit standing, credit capacity, general reputation, or personal characteristics.

consumer reporting agency Any person or organization that regularly prepares consumer reports and furnishes them, either for profit or on a cooperative, nonprofit basis, to other persons or organizations. Also called a *credit reporting agency.* See also *Fair Credit Reporting Act (FCRA).*

contestable period The period of time (usually two years) during which an insurer may challenge the validity of a life insurance policy. See also *incontestable clause.*

contested claim See *resisted claim.*

contingencies Unexpected events that cause actual expenses, investment earnings, mortality rates, morbidity rates, or persistency rates to depart significantly from company forecasts or assumptions.

contingency reserves Statutory reserves created by U.S. insurers as a cushion against various special risks. Also called *appropriated surplus, assigned surplus, earmarked surplus,* and *special surplus.*

contingent beneficiary The party designated to receive life insurance policy proceeds if the primary beneficiary should die before the person whose life is insured dies. Also called the *secondary beneficiary* or the *successor beneficiary.*

contingent owner See *successor owner.*

contingent payee The party who will receive any life insurance or annuity proceeds that are still payable at the time of the primary payee's death. Also called the *successor payee.*

contingent payment A payment that will be made only if some predesignated condition is met, such as the recipient being alive.

continuance table A type of morbidity table showing the proportion of disabilities that are expected to last various lengths of time; used by insurers to help forecast the length of a disability.

continuous-premium whole life insurance   Whole life insurance for which premiums are payable throughout the life of the policy. Also called *straight life insurance.*

contractholder See *contractowner.*

contract of adhesion   A legally binding agreement that is prepared by one party and that must be accepted or rejected as a whole by the other party, without any bargaining between the parties to the agreement. Insurance contracts are contracts of adhesion.

contract of indemnity   A type of contract in which the amount of the benefit to be paid is based on the actual amount of financial loss as determined at the time of loss. For example, many health insurance contracts are contracts of indemnity. See also *valued contract.*

contractowner   The person who applies for and purchases an individual annuity contract. See also *annuitant.*

contributed surplus   On a Canadian life insurance company's balance sheet, the amount in excess of par value paid in by stockholders minus the amount of dividends paid to stockholders.

contribution limit   The maximum annual addition permitted by law to be made to a participant's account in a defined contribution pension plan. The annual contribution includes employer contributions, employee contributions, and forfeitures that have been reallocated from other participants' accounts. The limit is subject to legislative change and is generally indexed to inflation so that it increases as price levels increase. In the United States, the contribution limit is set under Section 415 of the Internal Revenue Code. See also *maximum benefit* and *Section 415 limits.*

contribution to surplus   In mutual insurance companies, the income that results when an insurance company makes more money than is needed to pay for the cost of providing insurance.

contributory group insurance Any group insurance plan that calls for the insureds to pay a portion of the cost of the group insurance coverage. Contrast to *noncontributory group insurance.*

contributory plan Any pension or employee benefit plan in which plan participants must make contributions to fund the plan. Contrast with *noncontributory plan.*

convention blank The standardized Annual Statement form that all United States insurers must complete and submit yearly to their state's insurance regulators. See *Annual Statement.*

conversion fund The fund in which unallocated employer contributions to a combination plan are accumulated. Also called a *side fund.*

conversion privilege (1) A group life insurance policy provision that allows a group insured whose coverage terminates for specified reasons to convert his group coverage to an individual policy of insurance without presenting evidence of his insurability. (2) The right to change insurance coverage in certain prescribed situations from one type of policy to another without presenting evidence of insurability. For example, the right to change from an individual term insurance policy to a permanent plan of insurance.

conversion provision A group medical expense insurance policy provision that grants an insured group member who is leaving the group a limited right to purchase an individual medical expense insurance policy without presenting evidence of her insurability.

convertible term insurance A type of term insurance that allows the policyowner to change the term insurance policy to a whole life policy without providing evidence of insurability.

cooperative advertising program An advertising arrangement in which the insurance company pays part of a distributor's cost to advertise in the distributor's local market.

coordination of benefits (COB) clause A group medical expense insurance policy provision that is designed to prevent a group member who is insured under more than one group insurance policy from receiving benefit amounts greater than his actual incurred medical expenses. See also *nonduplication of benefits provision* and *overinsurance provision.*

copayment A flat amount that a medical plan member must pay at the time or service for certain medical services, such as office visits or prescription drugs.

corridor (1) In the United States, the required difference between a universal life insurance policy's face amount and the policy's cash value. This difference is a specified percentage that depends on the insured's age. If a policy's cash value exceeds the required percentage of the face amount (that is, intrudes on the corridor), the policy will be considered an investment contract rather than an insurance contract. Also called the *TEFRA corridor.* (2) In reinsurance, an amount of insurance which is in excess of the ceding company's retention limit but which is less than the reinsurer's minimum cession. The ceding company must usually retain this amount of insurance.

corridor deductible A flat amount that an insured must pay above the amount paid by his or her hospital-surgical expense policy before any benefits are payable under the major medical policy. In a sense, the deductible bridges the gap between a hospital-surgical policy and a major medical policy.

cost comparison methods The different formulas that insurance companies use to show prospective policyowners the cost of different insurance policies. See also *company retention method, interest-adjusted net cost (IANC) method,* and *rate of return method.*

cost-of-living adjustment (COLA) An increase in a pension benefit, disability income benefit or life income benefit to compensate for an increase in the cost of living. See also *indexation.*

coupon advertisement As defined by the Superintendent's Guidelines in Canada, (1) a sales inducement designed to invite the public to contract for insurance by the inclusion of an application for an individual insurance contract or (2) a broad description of coverage designed to invite the public to request an application for insurance with additional printed material for the purpose of issuing the applicant an individual insurance contract.

CPP See *Canada Pension Plan (CPP)*.

credentialing The process of reviewing applications of potential providers to be sure that they meet the criteria established by a managed care organization, and maintaining or verifying information on licenses, board certification, education, and work experience credentials, hospital privileges, and malpractice history and insurance.

credibility The amount of credit or weight given to a group's actual claims experience in projecting future claims or in calculating an experience refund. See also *experience rating* and *experience refund*.

crediting rate The interest that an insurer pays its customers in a given time period on interest-sensitive products.

crediting-rate resolution A formal declaration by a company's board of directors of the rate of interest that an insurer will credit on customers' money held in interest-sensitive products. Also known as a *crediting resolution*, an *interest resolution*, or an *interest-rate resolution*.

credit life insurance A type of decreasing term insurance designed to pay the balance due on a loan if the borrower dies before the loan is repaid.

credit reporting agency See *consumer reporting agency*.

credits In the numerical rating system, credits represent underwriting factors that have a favorable effect on an individual's mortality rating. Credits are assigned negative values. See also *debits* and *numerical rating system*.

cross-purchase method A method of purchasing a deceased partner's interest in a partnership in which each partner agrees to purchase a proportionate share of a deceased partner's interest. See also *entity method.*

cross-selling The process of selling both property/casualty and life and health insurance, as well as other financial services products, to the same customer.

CRVM See *Commissioners Reserve Valuation Method (CRVM).*

current assumption whole life insurance See *interest-sensitive whole life insurance.*

current settlement option rates Settlement option rates that reflect the interest rates currently earned by the insurer.

curtailment An event or amendment to a pension plan that significantly reduces plan benefits or employer contributions. Types of curtailments include a reduction of the expected years of future service of present employees, and the elimination of the accrual of defined benefits for some or all of the future services of a significant number of employees.

customer service department The department in a life and health insurance company that is charged with providing assistance to the company's policyowners, agents, and beneficiaries. Customer service specialists answer policyowners' requests for information, help them interpret policy language, answer questions about policy coverage, and make changes requested by the policyowner, such as changing the policyowner's address, beneficiary designation, and mode of premium payment. The customer service department may also send premium notices to customers, collect premium payments, and calculate and process policy loans, nonforfeiture options, dividends, and surrenders. In some companies, the customer service department also processes commission payments for company agents. Also called the *client service department,* the *policy administration department,* the *policyowner service department,* and the *service and claim department.*

cut-off A termination provision of a reinsurance agreement by virtue of which the reinsurer is not liable for losses covered by reinsured policies in force on the date of termination if the losses occur after the date of termination. Contrast to *run-off.*

dating back See *back-dating.*

DCI form See *duplicate coverage inquiry (DCI) form.*

death benefit The amount of money paid or due to be paid when a person insured under a life insurance policy dies. This amount does not include adjustments for outstanding policy loans, dividends, paid-up additions, or late premium payments. See also *basic death benefit* and *policy proceeds.*

death claim A request for payment under the terms of a life insurance policy.

debit See *territory.*

debit agents See *home service agents.*

debiting In the home service distribution system, charging an agent with the amount of premiums to be collected in that agent's territory.

debits In the numerical rating system, debits represent underwriting factors that have an unfavorable effect on an individual's mortality rating. Debits are assigned positive values. See also *credits* and *numerical rating system.*

debtor-creditor groups A group composed of lending institutions— banks, credit unions, savings and loan associations, finance companies, retail merchants, and credit card companies—and their debtors. See also *group creditor life insurance.*

declined risks The risk category that is composed of proposed insureds who are considered to present a risk that is too great for the insurer to cover.

decreasing term insurance A type of term life insurance in which the amount of coverage decreases during the term of coverage.

decrement A reduction in the number of participants in a pension plan caused by factors such as retirement, disability, death, or termination.

deductible A flat amount of covered medical expenses that an insured must incur before the insurer will make any benefit payments under a medical expense policy. Also called the *deductible amount* or *initial deductible*. See also *calendar year deductible, corridor deductible, family deductible, integrated deductible* and *per cause deductible*.

deferral date A date some time after the first anniversary of a group insurance policy to which an insurance company defers the payment of the policy's first renewal premium. An insurance company might defer this payment so that it could use the full first year's experience to help calculate the new premium.

deferred annuity An annuity contract under which premiums are accumulated at interest and the annuity income benefits begin more than one annuity period after the date on which the annuity is purchased. See also *deferred life annuity* and *group deferred annuity*.

deferred compensation plan A plan established by an employer to provide benefits to an employee at a later date, such as after the employee's retirement.

deferred life annuity A deferred annuity that provides a series of payments, each of which is made only if a designated person is alive.

deferred premium arrangement See *premium-delay arrangement*.

deferred premiums Premiums that are due after an insurer's Annual Statement date but before the next policy anniversary.

Deferred Profit Sharing Plan (DPSP) In Canada, a profit sharing plan that qualifies for favorable tax treatment. See also *profit-sharing plan.*

defined benefit formula A formula used to determine the periodic payment amounts that each participant in a defined benefit pension plan will receive at retirement. The benefit amount is often related to number of years of participation in the plan.

defined benefit pension plan A pension plan that specifies the benefits that the plan promises to pay to a participant upon retirement, with the benefits determined according to a specified formula. Contrast with *defined contribution pension plan.*

defined contribution formula A formula that describes the amount of money that will be deposited into a pension plan each year on behalf of each plan participant. Usually, the contribution is a specified percentage of the participant's compensation.

defined contribution pension plan A pension plan that specifies the amount of annual contributions that the plan sponsor will make on behalf of a plan participant. A defined contribution plan does not guarantee a specific amount of retirement benefits. A participant's benefits at retirement are based on the amount that has been contributed to the participant's account, plus investment earnings. Contrast with *defined benefit pension plan.*

delay clause See *common disaster clause.*

demutualization The process of converting a mutual insurance company to a stock insurance company.

dental expense coverage Insurance that provides benefits for routine dental examinations, preventive dental work, and dental procedures needed to treat tooth decay and diseases of the teeth and jaw.

dental health maintenance organization (DHMO) A managed care organization that provides dental services to its members in return for a fixed, prepaid fee.

dentist-consultant A licensed dentist who understands the underwriting intent of dental plan language as well as the accepted standards of dental practice, and who advises insurers as to the appropriateness of dental treatment.

dependent life insurance Group life insurance made available to group members, usually on an optional and contributory basis, to cover the spouse, children, or other dependents of the group member. It is usually sold in small amounts which are intended to pay funeral expenses.

deposit administration contract A funding vehicle for a pension plan in which the plan sponsor places plan assets in an insurance company's general account. When a plan participant retires, the insurer withdraws sufficient funds from the general account to buy an immediate annuity for the plan participant. A deposit administration contract usually protects the plan sponsor against investment loss and guarantees minimum investment returns. Also called a *group deposit administration contract.* See also *immediate annuity* and *immediate participation guarantee (IPG) contract.*

deposit term insurance A type of level term insurance that requires a substantially larger premium payment in the first year than the amount of level annual premiums payable in subsequent years.

detached agent An insurance agent who works out of personal offices located in or close to the agent's home, rather than in one of the insurer's field offices. See also *insurance agent.*

determination letter In the United States, a ruling by the Internal Revenue Service (IRS) as to whether the design of a pension plan satisfies the criteria necessary for the plan to be a qualified plan.

development allowances See *training allowances.*

development expenses The costs of planning and creating insurance products.

deviated rate   In group creditor insurance in the United States, a premium rate for a contributory plan that is higher than the prima facie rate and based on the group's actual claims experience. Insurers can charge a deviated rate only after the prima facie rate has been in effect for a certain period of time and only after being granted permission by the state insurance commissioner. Contrast with *prima facie rate.*

DHMO   See *dental health maintenance organization (DHMO).*

diagnostic related groups (DRGs)   In the United States, a prospective payment method used in the Medicare Program in which payment is not based on the number and kinds of medical services that a patient receives, but instead is based on the diagnosis of each patient.

direct-contract HMO   A type of open panel HMO that contracts directly with physicians who agree to provide medical services for HMO members. See *open-panel HMO.*

direct insurer   See *ceding company.*

direct mail   In insurance, printed solicitations that are addressed directly to prospective purchasers of insurance products.

direct response distribution system   In insurance, a distribution system that relies on advertisements, telephone solicitations, and mailings to generate sales. The advertisements and solicitations generally inform the customer how to apply for the insurance or how to contact the insurer.

direct response marketing   A method of selling insurance products, usually through direct mail, advertising in print and broadcast media, or by telephone solicitation.

direct writer   See *ceding company.*

direct writing company   See *ceding company.*

disability Inability to work due to an injury or sickness. See also *partial disability, presumptive disability,* and *total disability.*

disability benefits Benefits that are payable periodically while an insured continues to be disabled. "Being disabled" is generally defined in terms of inability to work. See also *total disability.*

disability buy-out insurance Insurance that provides cash funds to a business or professional partnership so that the business interests of a totally disabled partner or stockholder may be purchased if the disability is long-term or permanent.

disability income benefit A supplementary life insurance policy benefit that provides a monthly income benefit to a policyowner-insured who becomes totally disabled.

disability income insurance A type of health insurance designed to compensate insured people for a portion of the income they lose because of a disabling injury or illness. Generally, benefits for disability income insurance are provided for the disabled person in the form of monthly payments. Sometimes called *loss of time insurance.* See also *long-term disability income insurance* and *short-term disability income insurance.*

disability table (1) A tabulation of the probabilities of becoming disabled at each age, plus certain related figures. (2) A tabulation of the number of persons who are still disabled at each age and the duration of disability, plus certain related figures.

disabled life annuity A series of payments, each of which is contingent on a person being alive and still disabled.

disabled life reserve A claim reserve liability that is the present value of all amounts that are predicted to become payable while an insured is disabled. See also *claim reserve.*

discharge planning A component of utilization review (UR) in which the UR staff, before the patient leaves the hospital, makes arrangements for at-home care, medical equipment and services, and other specific needs the patient may have upon discharge from the hospital.

discharge provision Part of a small estates statute which releases an insurance company from liability under an insurance contract if it pays the proceeds to the deceased insured's estate. See *small estates statutes.*

Discontinuity Index A test required by the NAIC Model Life Insurance Disclosure Regulation and designed to disclose instances in which policy illustrations have been manipulated so that they present an unrealistic progression of premiums, dividends, and benefits.

discounted fee-for-service payment structure A fee structure used by some HMOs under which the HMO pays physicians a certain percentage of their normal fees, thereby achieving a "discount" on those fees.

discretionary costs Costs that are partially or wholly under the control of current management and are flexible components of an insurer's budget.

discretionary group According to the NAIC Group Health Insurance Model Act, a group that is not an employer, a creditor, a labor union, a trust established by an employer or union, an association, or a credit union, but that the commissioner of insurance believes is in the public interest and, therefore, is eligible to purchase a group health insurance contract.

disintermediation The process of removing money from a financial intermediary in order to earn a higher yield somewhere else, usually with another financial intermediary. Historically, disintermediation, through policy loans or surrendered policies, has been a major problem for life and health insurers during periods of economic depression and high inflation.

disputed claim See *resisted claim.*

distress termination In pension and employee-benefit plans, the curtailment of a plan which does not have sufficient funds to cover all the benefits to which the plan's participants are entitled. Contrast to *standard plan termination.* See also *involuntary plan termination* and *voluntary plan termination.*

distribution expenses Expenses involved in making insurance products available to the general public. These expenses include agent compensation, group sales representatives' salaries, and postal, printing, and telecommunications expenses for those companies that use direct response marketing.

distribution of risk See *good distribution of risk.*

distribution system A method of transferring products from the insurance company to the consumer.

dividend (1) A refund of excess premium paid to the owner of an individual participating life insurance policy. Such a dividend is paid out of an insurer's divisible surplus. Also called a *policy dividend* or a *policyowner dividend.* See also *divisible surplus.* (2) The portion of a group insurance premium that is returned to a group policyholder whose claims experience is better than had been expected when the premium was calculated. Also called *experience rating refund, experience refund,* and *retroactive rate reduction.* (3) A periodic payment paid by a business to a stockholder. A dividend paid in cash is called a *cash dividend.* A dividend paid in the form of additional shares of stock is called a *stock dividend.*

dividend accumulations Amounts that result when a policyowner decides to leave policy dividends on deposit with an insurer. Also called *dividend credits.*

dividend additions See *paid-up additions.*

dividend credits See *dividend accumulations.*

dividend expenses   When an insurer calculates policyowner dividends, dividend expenses represent the amount of money that it costs the insurer to maintain each policy in force for the current year.

dividend liability   A liability account representing policy dividends and experience rating refunds that have been declared but that have not yet been paid.

dividend interest rate   The interest rate that represents the actual rate being earned on an insurer's present investments. The dividend interest rate is used to calculate policyowner dividends.

dividend options   Several alternatives that participating policyowners can choose from to indicate the manner in which they want to receive their share of the insurance company's divisible surplus. See *accumulation at interest dividend option, additional term insurance dividend option, automatic dividend option, cash payment dividend option, dividend accumulations, enhancement type policy, paid-up additions,* and *premium reduction dividend option.*

dividend rate of mortality   The rate of mortality (for a given age) that an insurer chooses to use in calculating policyowner dividends. The dividend rate of mortality is the mortality rate currently experienced by the insurer on the policies it has sold.

divisible surplus   The portion of an insurer's surplus, set aside annually from current earnings, and earmarked for distribution to owners of participating policies. See also *surplus.*

doctrine of reasonable expectations   A doctrine applied by some courts under which the reasonable expectations of policyowners and beneficiaries will be honored, even though the language of the policy does not literally support these expectations.

domestic insurer   From the point of view of a particular state in the United States, an insurer incorporated under the laws of that state. Compare to *alien insurer* and *foreign insurer.*

double indemnity An accidental death benefit that is equal to the face amount of the life insurance policy. See also *accidental death benefit (ADB) rider.*

DPSP See *Deferred Profit Sharing Plan (DPSP).*

dread disease (DD) benefit An accelerated death benefit provided by some individual life insurance policies under which the insurer agrees to pay a portion of the policy's face amount before the policyowner-insured dies if the policyowner-insured suffers from one of a number of specified diseases.

dread disease coverage A type of medical expense policy designed to cover only those medical expenses caused by a specified disease, such as cancer, which is named in the policy. Also called a *limited coverage policy.*

DRGs See *diagnostic related groups (DRGs).*

DST See *dynamic solvency testing (DST).*

drinking criticism An underwriting term for evidence of alcohol abuse or alcoholism.

dual-choice provision In the United States, part of the Health Maintenance Organization Act of 1973 which requires employers that meet certain specifications to offer health insurance through a federally qualified HMO as an alternative to a traditional health insurance plan.

dual registration The licensing of registered representatives with more than one broker-dealer.

due and unpaid claims Claims that have been approved by an insurer but that have not yet been paid.

due income Income that was due to be received prior to the financial reporting date but that has not been received by the insurer as of the reporting date.

duplicate coverage inquiry (DCI) form   In the United States, a form filled out by a health insurance company claim office and sent to another company in order to ascertain whether an accident or injury for which the first company has received a claim is also insured by the second company.

dynamic solvency testing (DST)   The use of simulation modeling to project into the future an insurance company's existing and future business in terms of assets, liabilities, and owners' equity.

E&O insurance   See *error and omissions (E&O) insurance.*

earlier birthday method   See *birthday rule.*

early retirement age   An age specified in a pension plan that is earlier than the plan's normal retirement age but at which a plan participant can still receive an immediate pension benefit. The benefit received at early retirement is usually actuarially reduced from the amount that would have been received had retirement occurred at the normal retirement age. See also *late retirement age* and *normal retirement age.*

earmarked surplus   See *special surplus fund.*

earned commission   See *conditionally vested commission.*

economic solvency   See *solvency.*

ELAD   See *equivalent level annual dividend (ELAD).*

election period   A 60-day period following notification of an insured's eligibility for COBRA continuation coverage, during which the individual can accept or decline the coverage.

elective contributions or **elective deferrals**   In the United States, contributions to an employee's Section 401(k) plan (cash or deferred arrangement) that are made by the employer on the employee's behalf. The contributions are made using before-tax dollars obtained through a voluntary reduction of the employee's salary. The contributions are tax-deferred to the employee. See also *matching contributions* and *nonelective contributions.*

electronic funds transfer (EFT) method An automatic premium payment technique whereby the policyowner authorizes her bank to withdraw funds from her account to pay each renewal premium.

eligibility period In contributory group insurance plans, the period of time, usually 31 days, during which a new group member may apply for group insurance coverage. Also called an *enrollment period.*

eligibility requirements The conditions a person must meet in order to be a participant in a group life insurance, group health insurance, or retirement plan.

elimination period See *waiting period.*

employee benefit plan A program under which an employer provides its employees with various benefits in addition to their wages.

employee benefits consultant A professional who helps employers analyze and design their employee benefit plans.

employee contribution See *percentage contribution.*

Employee Retirement Income Security Act of 1974 (ERISA) A United States federal law establishing (a) the rights of pension plan participants, (b) standards for the investment of pension plan assets, and (c) requirements for the disclosure of plan provisions and funding. ERISA also established the Pension Benefit Guaranty Corporation (PBGC).

employee's cost basis In the United States, an amount that is subtracted from the total amount of a distribution to a pension plan participant in order to determine the portion of the distribution that is subject to federal taxation. The cost basis is the amount on which an employee has already been taxed. It includes the amount of the nondeductible contributions made to the plan by the participant, any cost of plan-provided life insurance that was reported as taxable income by the participant, and other factors, including the amount of any employer contributions previously taxed as income to the participant.

Employees Profit Sharing Plan (EPSP) In Canada, a type of profit sharing plan to which the employer and employees generally contribute. For tax purposes, the employer may deduct the amount it deposits. Employees are generally taxed on contributions on their behalf in the year the contributions are made and on interest earnings when they are earned, but are not taxed when they leave the plan and receive the benefits. There are few limitations on the size of the contributions employers may make or on the ways that plan funds may be invested.

employee stock ownership plan (ESOP) Generally, any qualified employee-benefit plan that invests some or all plan assets in employer stock. In the United States, ERISA further defines an ESOP as either a qualified stock bonus plan or a combination qualified stock bonus plan and defined contribution pension plan designed to invest primarily in employer securities. The employer's contributions are tax deductible for the employer and tax deferred for the employee.

endorsement See *rider.*

endorsement method (1) A method by which the owner of a life insurance or an annuity policy may transfer all ownership rights in the policy to another party by notifying the insurer in writing of the change. (2) A change of beneficiary procedure that requires the name of the new beneficiary to be added to the policy itself by means of an endorsement in order for the beneficiary change to be effective. Contrast with *recording method.*

endowment insurance A type of life insurance that provides a benefit (a) if death occurs during the term of coverage or (b) if, at the end of the term of coverage, the insured is alive.

English rule A general rule of law stating that if several assignees notify an insurer of the assignment of a life insurance or annuity policy, the assignee with priority to the policy proceeds is the assignee who first notifies the insurer of the assignment. See also *American rule.*

enhancement type policy A life insurance policy in which part of each dividend provides paid-up additions, while the other part provides one-year term insurance to produce a predetermined total death benefit.

enrolled actuary In the United States, a pension actuary who meets the standards of, and is enrolled by, the federal agency known as the Joint Board for the Enrollment of Actuaries.

enrollment period See *eligibility period.*

entire contract provision A provision contained in life insurance and annuity policies to define the documents that constitute the entire insurance contract. These documents are the policy itself, the application that is attached to the policy, and any riders that are attached to the policy.

entity method A method of purchasing a deceased partner's interest in a partnership in which the partnership agrees to purchase the interest and to distribute a proportionate share of that ownership interest to each surviving partner. See also *cross-purchase method.*

EOB statement See *explanation of benefits (EOB) statement.*

EPO See *exclusive provider organization (EPO).*

EPSP See *Employees Profit Sharing Plan (EPSP).*

equitable assignment An assignment that does not meet the requirements of a legal assignment but which will be enforced in an equitable action if fairness so requires.

equity-based insurance product A life insurance or annuity product in which the cash value and benefit level fluctuate according to the performance of a portfolio of equity investments. The owners of this type of insurance product accept the risk of sharing in the insurer's investment gains and losses. Equity investments are investments by virtue of which investors gain part ownership in a corporation. The primary type of equity investment is corporate stock. See also *variable annuity, variable life insurance,* and *variable universal life insurance.*

equity pension A pension that provides benefit amounts which, at least in part, vary in accordance with the investment results of a portfolio of common stocks and other investment vehicles. The equity portion of the pension benefit is meant to provide retirees with benefits that increase as inflation rises.

equivalent level annual dividend (ELAD) One amount presented to consumers as part of the interest-adjusted method of comparing the costs of life insurance policies. The equivalent level annual dividend is meant to represent the part of the interest-adjusted payment and the cost that is, in effect, not guaranteed by the insurer, because dividends will change in the future as the insurer's experience changes. This amount gives the buyer an indication of the extent to which these nonguaranteed amounts affect the interest-adjusted payment and the cost of a policy.

equivalent single payment One payment that can replace several other payments, because it equals the value of the other payments.

equivocal suicide An apparent suicide in which there is doubt about whether the deceased intended to die as a result of an apparently self-destructive act.

ERISA See *Employee Retirement Income Security Act of 1974 (ERISA).*

error and omissions (E&O) insurance Insurance designed to cover claims that result from the negligent acts or mistakes of an agent, including (1) his or her vicarious liability stemming from negligent acts or (2) mistakes committed by individuals for whom the agent is legally liable.

escheat laws See *unclaimed property statutes.*

ESOP See *employee stock ownership plan (ESOP).*

estate plan A plan that addresses how best to preserve an individual's assets after the individual dies. Life insurance is often an important part of an estate plan.

estate planning department See *advanced underwriting department.*

evidence of insurability Proof that a person is an insurable risk.

excess interest The amount of interest above the guaranteed amount that an insurance company pays on a settlement option when interest rates are high.

excess-of-loss reinsurance plan The type of excess reinsurance plan most often used in health insurance. The reinsurer is usually liable if a specific claim exceeds a certain limit, called the attachment point.

excess reinsurance plan A type of reinsurance plan in which the reinsurer pays claims only in excess of a specified amount that may be related to losses per insured person, losses per accident or event, or total losses per class of business.

exchange program A program that allows a proposed insured who is replacing a policy to obtain the new policy on the basis of little or no evidence of insurability if his or her insurability has recently been established by the company that issued the original policy.

exclusion rider An attachment to a health insurance policy that excludes or limits coverage for a specific health impairment. Also called *impairment rider* or *impairment waiver.*

exclusions Losses for which an insurance policy does not provide benefits. For life insurance and accidental death benefit coverages, exclusions describe causes of death for which benefits will not be paid. In health insurance policies, exclusions describe losses not covered, such as those related to pre-existing conditions, cosmetic surgery, or self-inflicted injuries.

exclusive agents   Career agents who are under contract with one insurance company only and who are not permitted to sell the products of other insurers. Also known as *captive agents.*

exclusive provider organization (EPO)   A managed care organization, similar to a *preferred provider organization (PPO)*, except that an EPO generally does not cover out-of-network care.

exclusive territory   Under the general agency distribution system, a territory in which no individual other than the general agent is permitted to offer the insurer's products. Compare to *nonexclusive territory* and *overlapping territory.*

exculpatory statute   Legislation in community-property states that allows an insurer to pay the proceeds of a life insurance policy in accordance with the terms of that policy without fear of double liability.

exoneration statutes   Statutes that excuse the insurer from liability if a party claims policy proceeds which the insurer has already paid to a third party in good faith and without knowledge of any conflicting claim.

expected mortality The number of deaths that have been predicted to occur in a group of people at a given age. Also known as *tabular mortality.* Contrast with *mortality experience.*

expense participation   A medical plan provision requiring the insured to share in the payment of incurred medical expenses.

expense ratio   A ratio that measures the percentage of health insurance expenses paid for each dollar of premium income.

experience gains or losses   In pension planning, experience gains or losses arise when the actual conditions under which a plan operated during a period did not match the actuarial assumptions underlying the plan's cost estimates. If actual experience was more favorable financially than had been assumed, an experience gain occurs. If actual experience was less favorable financially than had been assumed, an experience loss occurs. Also known as *actuarial gains or losses.*

experience-premium method A method for calculating dividends wherein a basic amount is calculated (the difference between the gross premium and the experience premium), to which is added the year's contribution from interest.

experience premiums Special annual premiums that are calculated using dividend rates of mortality and expenses but tabular rates of interest.

experience rating A method of setting group insurance premium rates under which the insurer considers the particular group's past experience. See also *blended rating* and *manual rating.*

experience refund (1) The portion of a group insurance premium that is returned to a group policyholder whose claims experience is better than had been expected when the premium was calculated. Also called a *dividend,* an *experience rating refund,* and a *retroactive rate reduction.* See also *dividend.* (2) The portion of a reinsurance premium that is returned to the ceding company when claims experience is better than had been expected when the premium was calculated.

experimental underwriting The practice of cautiously accepting specific types of risk that are considered uninsurable according to the insurer's normal underwriting guidelines.

explanation of benefits (EOB) statement A statement from an insurer giving specific details to an insured group member about how and why benefit payments were or were not made.

express authority The authority that a principal explicitly confers on an agent. See *agent* and *principal.* Compare to *apparent authority* and *implied authority.*

extended spouse's allowance In Canada, an Old Age Security (OAS) benefit payable to a person who has been receiving a spouse's allowance and whose spouse dies. The benefit is payable until the recipient reaches age 65 or remarries. See also *spouse's allowance.*

extended term insurance option A nonforfeiture option in which the net cash value of a policy is applied as a net single premium to purchase paid-up term insurance. The amount of term insurance is equal to the death benefit of the policy being surrendered less any outstanding policy loans. The insured maintains the same amount of coverage but usually for a shorter period of time than the original coverage. See also *nonforfeiture options.*

extra-percentage tables method A commonly used plan for rating substandard risks. Under this method, each substandard class is charged a premium rate that is a certain percentage above the standard premium rate. Contrast with *flat extra premium method.*

face amount In a life insurance policy in which the benefit is not variable, the amount stated as payable at the death of the insured. It is generally shown on the first page of the policy. Also called the *face value.* See also *basic death benefit, death benefit,* and *policy proceeds.*

face page The first page of an insurance policy. The face page normally includes the insured's name and age, the name of the policyowner (if different from the insured's name), the amount of premiums, the policy number, the date on which the policy was issued, and the signatures of the insurance company's president and secretary.

face value See *face amount.*

facility-of-payment clause A life insurance policy provision that permits an insurer to pay all or part of the policy proceeds either to a blood relative of the insured or to anyone who has a valid claim to those proceeds. The facility-of-payment clause enables the insurer to pay benefits in a timely manner when such benefits cannot be made to the beneficiary identified in the insurance contract.

fac-ob reinsurance treaty   See *facultative-obligatory (fac-ob) reinsurance treaty*.

factor table   A table used by insurance underwriters to determine an applicant's net worth by specifying what an applicant's annual income should be multiplied by to arrive at the maximum allowable amount of insurance.

facultative-obligatory (fac-ob) reinsurance treaty   A type of reinsurance agreement that combines the features of automatic and facultative treaties. Under a fac-ob treaty, the ceding company does all the case underwriting on the risks to be reinsured, sending no underwriting papers to the reinsurer. The facultative aspect of the fac-ob treaty is that the ceding company is sending only selected risks to the reinsurer, rather than all the risks, as with an automatic treaty. The automatic, or obligatory, aspect of the fac-ob treaty is that the reinsurer is obligated to accept submitted risks unless it does not have the retention capacity to cover the risks submitted.

facultative reinsurance treaty   A reinsurance treaty under which the ceding company chooses the individual applications it wants to submit for reinsurance and the reinsurer can choose the risks it wishes to accept rather than being bound to accept risks as under an automatic treaty. The reinsurer may also apply its own ratings to the risks it accepts.

Fair Credit Reporting Act (FCRA)   A United States federal law designed to help ensure that consumer reporting agencies act fairly, impartially, and with respect for the consumer's right to privacy when preparing consumer reports on individuals. See also *consumer reporting agency*.

family benefit   A life insurance policy rider that provides term insurance coverage on the insured's spouse and children.

family deductible   A single deductible that, when satisfied, relieves a family of the burden of satisfying a deductible for each individual family member.

family income coverage Decreasing term life insurance that provides a stated monthly income benefit to the insured's surviving spouse if the insured dies during the term of coverage. Monthly income benefits continue until the end of the term specified when the coverage was purchased.

family insurance policy A whole life insurance policy that provides term insurance coverage on the insured's spouse and children.

FASB Statement No. 35 Issued in the United States by the Financial Accounting Standards Board (FASB) in 1985, Statement 35 contains rules by which to measure and report a defined benefit pension plan's assets and liabilities in accounting reports that are issued by the pension plan itself. The Statement is titled "Accounting and Reporting by Defined Benefit Plans."

FASB Statement No. 87 Issued in the United States by the Financial Accounting Standards Board (FASB) in 1985, Statement 87 governs the ways in which an employer accounts for and reports the costs of pension benefits offered to its employees. The Statement, titled "Employers' Accounting for Pensions," requires that, for accounting purposes, employers use a cost method known as the projected unit credit method to determine the net periodic cost of the pension benefits offered to employees. Statement 87 also requires that an employer recognize a liability if the net periodic cost is greater than employer contributions to the plan, and an asset if net periodic cost is less than employer contributions to the plan. An employer must also recognize a liability known as the unfunded accumulated benefit obligation if the accumulated obligations of the plan sponsored by the employer exceed the fair market value of the plan's assets.

FASB Statement No. 88 Issued in the United States by the Financial Accounting Standards Board (FASB) in 1985, Statement 88 establishes accounting requirements for employers whose defined benefit pension plans are curtailed or terminated, or experience other special events, such as a settlement of a pension obligation through a lump-sum cash payment of benefits to a plan participant. The Statement is titled "Employers' Accounting For Settlements and Curtailments of Defined Benefit Pension Plans and Termination Benefits."

FAST system See *Financial Analysis and Solvency Tracking (FAST) system.*

FCRA See *Fair Credit Reporting Act (FCRA).*

federally qualified HMO In the United States, a health maintenance organization (HMO) that satisfies specific requirements set forth in the Health Maintenance Organization Act of 1973. Federally qualified HMOs are entitled to certain grants and loans from the federal government and are eligible to be used by employers to satisfy the dual choice provision.

fee-for-service A system used by traditional medical expense insurance in which the insurer either reimburses the group member or pays the provider directly for each covered medical expense after the expense has been incurred. The insurer usually pays the provider's standard fee, so long as it does not exceed the *usual, customary, and reasonable (UCR) fee.*

fee schedule A schedule or list of maximum benefits that will be paid under a group medical contract for certain listed procedures. See also *relative value schedule.* May simply be called a *schedule.*

fee schedule payment structure A compensation plan used in health maintenance organizations (HMOs) and preferred provider organizations (PPOs) in which a physician is paid a predetermined amount for each service that the physician provides. See also *capitation.*

fiduciary A person or organization who holds, manages and has discretionary authority and control over money belonging to another person or organization, or who renders investment advice in exchange for compensation. When an insurance company manages pension funds, the insurance company is acting as a fiduciary.

field advisory council A group of agents established to provide feedback from an agency force in areas such as product design, rate setting, underwriting philosophy, and customer service.

field force Those insurance agents who work out of an insurer's field offices.

field office An insurance company's local sales office.

field underwriter See *insurance agent.*

field underwriting The first step in the risk selection process. Field underwriting occurs when an agent gathers pertinent information about the proposed insured and reports that information on the application blank so the home office underwriter can make an underwriting decision.

fifth dividend option See *additional term insurance dividend option.*

filing method See *recording method.*

final average (final earnings) benefit formula A type of defined-benefit formula in which the retirement benefit amount is derived on the basis of a participant's average compensation during a specified period (usually the three to five years preceding retirement) during which the participant was most highly compensated. Contrast with *career average (career earnings) benefit formula.*

final premium See *average premium.*

Financial Analysis and Solvency Tracking (FAST) system. In the United States, a system used by the NAIC to evaluate financial statement information in order to determine an insurer's financial condition.

financial institution An organization that helps channel funds through an economy by accepting the surplus money of savers and supplying that money to borrowers, who pay to use the money. Insurance companies are financial institutions.

financial intermediary A financial institution that borrows money on its own account and loans money to other borrowers. Insurance companies are financial intermediaries.

financial planning See *total-needs programming*.

financial reinsurance Reinsurance primarily designed to serve some financial or business purpose of one or both of the companies that are party to the agreement. For example, a financial reinsurance transaction can improve the profit or surplus of the ceding company or aid the company's tax planning. See *surplus relief*.

financial services industry The financial institutions that help consumers and business organizations save, borrow, invest, and otherwise manage money.

financial settlement A lump sum payment by an insurer to a disabled insured that extinguishes the insurer's responsibility under the disability contract. Also known as a *buy-out* or *commutation*.

first beneficiary See *primary beneficiary*.

first excess See *first surplus*.

first surplus In a layered reinsurance agreement, the amount of risk ceded in the first layer. See *layering*. Also called *first excess*.

first-dollar coverage Medical expense insurance under which no deductible or coinsurance is applicable to covered expenses.

first-to-die life insurance See *joint whole life insurance*.

first-year commission An amount paid to an insurance agent based on a policy's first annual premium amount.

501(c)(9) trust In the United States, a type of trust that many self-insured groups establish to fund their group insurance plans. All contributions to a 501(c)(9) trust are deductible for federal income tax purposes, as are all investment gains made on funds in the trust. The trust must meet certain federal government requirements. Also called a *voluntary employees' beneficiary association (VEBA)*. See also *self-insured group insurance plan*.

fixed amount option   A life insurance settlement option under which the insurer uses the policy proceeds plus interest to pay the beneficiary a sum of money in a series of equal installments for as long as the proceeds plus interest last. Also called the *fixed payment option*.

fixed period option   A life insurance settlement option under which the insurer pays the beneficiary the policy proceeds plus interest in a series of equal installments for a specified length of time.

flat amount formula   A method of determining the retirement benefit for participants in a defined benefit pension plan. A flat amount formula provides the same periodic (e.g., monthly, annual) benefit amount, for example $500 per month, to each retiree. See also *flat percentage of earnings formula* and *unit-benefit formula*.

flat extra premium method   A method for rating substandard risks used when the extra risk is considered to be constant. The underwriter assesses a specific extra premium for each $1,000 of insurance. Contrast with *extra-percentage tables method*.

flat percentage of earnings formula   A method of determining the retirement benefit for participants in a defined benefit pension plan. This method provides for each participant to receive a certain percentage of pre-retirement compensation, for example 60%. The actual payment amount under this formula depends on how compensation is defined. See also *career average benefit formula, final average benefit formula, flat amount formula,* and *unit-benefit formula*.

flexible benefit plan   See *cafeteria plan*.

flexible premium annuity   A deferred annuity for which the contractowner pays periodic premiums that may vary between a set minimum and a set maximum amount. The contractowner may also elect not to make any premium payment in any given period.

flexible premium life insurance See *indeterminate premium life insurance.*

flexible premium variable life insurance See *variable universal life insurance.*

flip-flop In reinsurance, a layering arrangement where the first two reinsurers agree to alternate the acceptance of the first and second layers of risk. Also called a *switch.* See *layering.*

foreign corporation In Canada, a non-Canadian insurance company that is incorporated under the laws of a country which is not a member of the British Commonwealth.

foreign insurer From the point of view of a particular state in the United States, an insurer that is incorporated under the laws of another state. Compare to *domestic insurer and alien insurer.*

foreseeability The ability of an insured to reasonably anticipate that harm or injury would most likely result from an act or absence of an act.

forfeiture The unvested amount that remains in a pension or profit sharing plan when a participant leaves the plan and withdraws the amounts which are vested. Forfeitures may occur when an employee is terminated, for example. Forfeitures must either be used to reduce the plan sponsor's future contributions to the plan or be reallocated to other participants.

Form 5500 See *Annual Report Form 5500.*

401(k) Plan See *Section 401(k) Plan.*

fractional premiums Premiums that are paid in installments during a year, such as semiannually, quarterly, or monthly. Fractional premiums are so called because they are fractions of the annual premium.

fraternal benefit society An organization that exists to provide social and insurance benefits to its members. In such a society, members often share a common religious, ethnic, or vocational background, although some fraternals are open to the general public.

fraternal insurance Insurance coverage issued by a fraternal benefit society. See also *open contract.*

fraudulent claim A type of claim that occurs when a claimant intentionally uses false information in an attempt to collect policy proceeds.

fraudulent misrepresentation According to common law, a false statement that meets the following three criteria: (1) the party that makes the statement is aware that it is not true or disregards whether it is true; (2) the party that makes the statement does so to induce another party to enter into a contract; (3) the other party does enter into a contract as a result of the statement and suffers a loss because of the contract.

free examination period The period of time after delivery of an insurance policy during which the policyowner may review the policy and return it to the company for a full refund of the initial premium. Full coverage is in force during this period. Also called a *ten-day free look.*

fronting In reinsurance, an arrangement whereby one insurer issues a policy on a risk for, and at the request of, one or more other insurers with the intent of ceding the entire risk to the other insurer or insurers.

fronting company The primary insurer in a fronting arrangement.

front-loaded policy A life insurance policy (usually a universal life insurance policy) in which most of the expense charges take the form of deductions from each premium payment. Such deductions continue throughout the premium payment period. See also *back-loaded policy* and *universal life insurance.*

70

full preliminary term method A modified reserving method according to which the first-year reserve is equal to the end-of-year reserve of a one-year term policy, which is $0.

full-service plan A health insurance plan that pays in full the actual cost, if reasonable and customary, of services received, rather than a specified maximum for each service.

fully contributory An arrangement in which the insureds under a group policy pay the entire cost of their insurance. Contrast with *contributory group insurance* and *noncontributory group insurance.*

fully-insured group insurance plan A form of group insurance in which an insurance company is financially responsible for paying claims made by group insureds. Contrast with *self-insured group insurance plan.*

functional cost analysis A company or agency cost control tool using data from many life and health insurance companies or agencies. For example, by using functional cost analysis, agency managers can compare the costs of specific agency operations, such as recruiting, manpower development, or sales, with the average costs of such operations in other agencies of the same size.

fund accounting The process used to account for and allocate revenue to various funds in Canadian insurance companies.

funding agency The party who holds the assets of a pension plan. Often an insurance company.

funding deficiency See *accumulated funding deficiency.*

funding instrument See *funding vehicle.*

funding standard account For qualified pension plans in the United States, a bookkeeping account that is maintained in order to determine whether a defined benefit pension plan is meeting minimum funding standards set by law. Many of the entries to the account are derived actuarially. If at any time the plan's funding is inadequate, then an accumulated funding deficiency is said to exist. Also known as a *minimum funding standard account.* See also *minimum funding standards.*

funding vehicle The means for investing a retirement plan's assets as they are accumulated. Also called the *funding instrument.*

future purchase option benefit A supplemental benefit that allows an insured to increase the benefit amount payable under a disability income policy in accordance with increases in the insured's earnings. Generally, the insured is not required to provide evidence of insurability to increase the benefit.

future service The prospective service that an employee will provide to an employer from the date of entry into a pension, or from the current date, to the employee's normal retirement date. Pension benefits provided for this service are known as future service benefits. See also *past service.*

GA See *general agent (GA).*

GAAP See *generally accepted accounting principles (GAAP).*

GAAP reserves Reserves that are calculated in accordance with generally accepted accounting principles.

gatekeeper A term used to describe the primary care physician's role in a managed care plan. This physican authorizes all services delivered to the insured by other physicians or health care providers.

gatekeeper PPO A preferred provider organization that requires each plan member to select a primary care physician who operates as a gatekeeper to control the member's utilization of medical care services.

general account An undivided account in which life and health insurers maintain funds from guaranteed insurance products such as ordinary life insurance. See also *separate account.*

general agent (GA) The individual in charge of an agency office. The general agent is an independent entrepreneur who is under contract to the insurer.

general asset group insurance plan A type of self-insured group health insurance plan under which the employer pays covered claims and expenses from its current operating funds. Also known as a *nontrusteed plan.*

general manager See *branch manager.*

generally accepted accounting principles (GAAP) A set of financial accounting standards that all U.S. stock companies and all Canadian companies follow when preparing financial statements.

GI benefit See *guaranteed insurability (GI) benefit.*

GIC See *guaranteed investment contract (GIC).*

GIO (guaranteed insurability option See *guaranteed insurability (GI) benefit.*

GIS See *Guaranteed Income Supplement (GIS).*

good distribution of risk In group insurance, the occurence, within a group, of a large number of preferred- and standard-risk individuals to offset the claims of the few substandard risks.

good health provision A provision contained in some group credit policies stating that a policy is void if the insured was not in good health when the application was signed or when the policy was delivered, whichever was specified in the contract.

GPM See *group practice model (GPM).*

grace period The length of time (usually 31 days) after a premium is due and unpaid during which the policy, including all riders, remains in force. If a premium is paid during the grace period, the premium is considered to have been paid on time.

grace period provision A policy provision that allows the policyowner to pay a renewal premium within a stated grace period following the renewal premium due date.

graded-premium whole life insurance A type of whole life insurance in which premiums increase at specified points in time, ultimately reaching a level premium amount payable for the remaining life of the policy. Graded-premium whole life generally features at least three levels of premium amounts.

gross premium The amount that policyowners actually pay for their insurance. The gross premium equals the net premium plus the loading.

group creditor life insurance Group term insurance that is issued to a creditor and covers the lives of the creditor's current and future debtors.

group deferred annuity A retirement plan funding vehicle under which contributions for each plan participant are used to purchase a series of single-premium deferred annuities.

group deposit administration contract See *deposit administration contract.*

group insurance Insurance that provides coverage for a number of people under one contract, called a master contract.

group life insureds In Canada, the persons who are insured by a group life insurance contract. Usually called "insureds" in the United States.

group-model HMO A type of closed-panel HMO that contracts with a group of physicians, who are usually employees of a physicians' group practice, to provide services to HMO members.

group ordinary life insurance Group life insurance in which at least a part of the coverage is permanent and builds a cash-value.

group paid-up insurance A type of contributory group life insurance in which the employee's contributions are used to purchase paid-up whole life insurance and the employer's contributions are used to purchase term insurance. The amount of insurance coverage on each employee remains level each year. Therefore, as the amount of paid-up insurance on an employee increases over time, the amount of term insurance that the employer must purchase to make up the difference decreases.

group permanent life insurance Any of several types of life insurance that build a cash value and are underwritten on a group basis. Group permanent life insurance is often used to fund group pension plans and/or to provide life insurance coverage that will continue after retirement.

group persons insured In Canada, the persons who are insured by a group health insurance contract. Usually called "insureds" in the United States.

group policyholder The employer or other party that enters into a group insurance contract with an insurer.

group practice model (GPM) A means of organizing a health maintenance organization (HMO) in which the physicians in the HMO share a central facility. See also *individual practice association (IPA).*

group representative A salaried insurance company employee who deals solely with the distribution of group insurance products. The primary responsibilities of group representatives include finding prospects, designing proposals, installing the product, and renegotiating the policy at renewal.

group RRSP In Canada, a collection of registered retirement savings plans (RRSPs) established and maintained by an employer in order to help employees save for retirement. Each RRSP within the group is owned entirely by the employee. Employer contributions, therefore, become vested as soon as they are made. All employer and employee contributions are deductible from the employee's taxable income.

group universal life insurance (GUL) Group life insurance for which the insured usually pays the full premium and can choose the amount of premium to pay, and in which the death benefit is determined by the amount of the premium. The insured can vary the premium and death benefit amounts during the life of the policy. Like individual universal life insurance, GUL is designed to combine insurance protection with a savings/investment element. In addition, GUL is usually "portable," which means that a group member who leaves the group can continue coverage under the group plan. Sometimes called a *Group Universal Life Program (GULP)*. See also *universal life insurance.*

guarantee In Canada, synonymous with *cession.*

guaranteed income contract See *guaranteed investment contract (GIC).*

Guaranteed Income Supplement (GIS) In Canada, a supplemental monthly benefit available to Old Age Security (OAS) recipients who receive less income than a stated amount.

guaranteed insurability (GI) benefit A supplementary life insurance policy benefit that gives the policyowner the right to purchase additional insurance of the same type as the basic policy without supplying evidence of the insured's insurability. Also known as *guaranteed insurability option (GIO).*

guaranteed interest contract See *guaranteed investment contract (GIC).*

guaranteed investment contract (GIC) A retirement plan funding vehicle under which the insurer accepts a single deposit from the plan sponsor and guarantees to pay a specified interest rate on the funds deposited during a specified time period. Also called a *guaranteed income contract* or a *guaranteed interest contract.*

guaranteed-issue insurance Insurance coverage for which there is usually no individual underwriting. All eligible members of a particular group of proposed insureds who apply for the policy and who meet certain conditions are automatically issued a policy.

guaranteed issue limit See *no-evidence limit.*

guaranteed renewable policy An individual health insurance policy that the insurer is required to renew—as long as premiums are paid—at least until the insured attains the age limit specified in the policy. The insurer may increase the premium rate for any class of guaranteed renewable policies. See also *cancellable policy, conditionally renewable policy, noncancellable and guaranteed renewable policy, noncancellable policy,* and *optionally renewable policy.*

guaranty association An association formed by life and health insurance companies to cover the financial obligations of member companies that fail.

guaranty-fund assessments Charges payable by sound insurers to support the customer obligations of a failed insurer that had operated in a jurisdiction where the surviving insurers conduct business.

Guidelines Governing Group Accident and Sickness Insurance In Canada, Superintendents' Guidelines that regulate several aspects of group health insurance contracts, including the types of groups to which a group health insurance contract may be issued and the particulars that must be included in the certificate issued to each person insured by the contract. See also *Superintendent's Guidelines.*

Guidelines Governing Group Life Insurance In Canada, a set of guidelines issued by the Canadian Council of Insurance Regulators. The guidelines specify, among other things, the types of groups eligible for group life insurance.

guide to buying life insurance In Canada, a written statement developed by the Canadian Life and Health Insurance Association (CLHIA). The guide describes the types of life insurance available, so that prospects for life insurance can compare the advantages and disadvantages of each type of policy.

GUL See *group universal life insurance (GUL).*

GULP (Group Universal Life Program) See *group universal life insurance (GUL).*

head office See *home office.*

health insurance Insurance covering medical expenses or income loss resulting from injury or sickness. Health insurance is a general category that includes many different types of insurance coverage, including hospital confinement insurance, hospital expense insurance, surgical expense insurance, major medical insurance, disability income insurance, dental expense insurance, prescription drug insurance, and vision care insurance. See also *disability income insurance* and *medical expense insurance.*

health maintenance organization (HMO) A health care financing and delivery system that provides comprehensive health care services for subscribing members in a particular geographic area in return for a fixed, prepaid fee. See also *group practice model (GPM)* and *individual practice association (IPA).*

heaped commission schedule See *levelized commission schedule.*

historical comparison A method designed to help an agency manager control and evaluate operating expenses by comparing the agency's current performance with its past performance.

history statement An Attending Physician's Statement concerning a specific health history admitted by the proposed insured.

HMO See *health maintenance organization (HMO).*

hold harmless release A discharge stating that a payee will reimburse an insurance company if a subsequent claimant successfully challenges the disbursement of the policy's proceeds.

home office The headquarters of an insurance company where the company's executive offices are usually located. Also known as the *head office.*

home-office-to-home-office arrangement A type of manufacturer-distributor arrangement in which an insurance company that chooses not to offer a particular product or product line agrees to act as a brokerage general agent for certain product lines manufactured by another insurer.

home service agents Exclusive or captive agents who work for home service companies and who collect premiums and provide service at the policyowner's residence. Home service agents offer monthly debit life, health, and fire insurance products as well as products for which premiums are billed by and remitted directly to the insurer. Some may also offer industrial insurance. Home service agents market products primarily to middle and lower-middle income individuals and families. See also *industrial insurance* and *monthly debit ordinary (MDO)*.

home service distribution system A distribution system that is used primarily for individual insurance products and that employs agents who collect premiums and provide service at the policyowner's residence. Each home service agent works within a defined geographical territory. See also *home service agents, industrial insurance,* and *monthly debit ordinary (MDO)*.

hospital confinement insurance A type of health insurance that provides a predetermined flat benefit amount for each day an insured is hospitalized. The benefit amount does not vary according to the amount of medical expenses the insured incurs, although some policies provide higher benefit amounts if the insured is in an intensive or cardiac care unit. Also called *hospital indemnity insurance.*

hospital expense insurance See *basic medical expense coverage.*

hospital indemnity insurance See *hospital confinement insurance.*

hospital-surgical expense insurance A type of health insurance that provides benefits related directly to hospitalization costs and associated medical expenses incurred by an insured for treatment of a sickness or injury. Most hospital-surgical expense policies cover (a) hospital charges for room, board, and hospital services, (b) surgeon's and physician's fees during a hospital stay, (c) specified outpatient expenses, and (d) extended care services, such as convalescent or nursing home costs.

hour of service As defined by ERISA in the United States, an hour for which an employee is entitled to be paid or is paid. An hour of service can be earned while the employee is performing services for the employer or during a period in which no service is performed due to vacation, holidays, illness, or other paid leaves of absence. See also *year of service.*

H.R. 10 plan See *Keogh plan.*

IANC See *interest-adjusted net cost (IANC) method.*

IBNR claims See *incurred but not reported claims.*

illness perils A classification used by health insurance underwriters to evaluate the type and degree of peril represented by a particular occupation. Illness perils include exposure to dust, poisons, and extreme temperatures. See also *accident perils.*

illustration See *sales illustration.*

immediate annuity An annuity under which income payments begin one period after the annuity is purchased. Often called a *single-premium immediate annuity (SPIA).*

immediate participation guarantee (IPG) contract A retirement plan funding vehicle under which the plan's assets are placed in the insurer's general investment account and are used to purchase an immediate annuity for each retired plan participant or to pay monthly benefits directly to retired participants. IPG contracts do not provide full guarantees against investment loss or guarantees regarding minimum investment returns. Instead, the plan sponsor shares in the gains or losses experienced by the life insurance company.

immediate underwriting A program used in some insurance companies to grant limited underwriting authority to certain agency or branch office managers in order to issue policies more quickly. Also called *underwriting at point of sale* or *point of sale underwriting.*

IMO See *independent marketing organization (IMO).*

impairment Any aspect of a proposed insured's health, occupation, activities, or lifestyle that could increase his or her expected mortality or morbidity.

impairment rider   See *exclusion rider.*

impairment waiver See *exlusion rider.*

implied authority The authority that a principal intends an agent to have and that arises incidentally from an express grant of authority. See *agent* and *principal.* Compare to *apparent authority* and *express authority.*

IMR See *interest maintenance reserve.*

incentive coinsurance provisions Provisions included in some dental policies that promote regular dental care by specifying that insurers will pay a higher percentage of dental expenses if the insured receives regular dental examinations.

incident of ownership Any policy right, including the right to (1) change the beneficiary, (2) cancel or surrender the policy, (3) assign the policy, (4) obtain a policy loan, or (5) use the policy as collateral for a loan.

income protection insurance A type of disability income policy which specifies that an insured is totally disabled and eligible to receive disability income benefits if that person suffers an income loss caused by a disability.

income replacement benefit   See *recovery benefit.*

income replacement ratio   The percentage of preretirement income that a retiree would need to receive after retirement in order to have a postretirement standard of living equivalent to his or her preretirement standard of living. This ratio is generally less than 100 percent, because some of an individual's expenses (i.e., taxes, commuting costs, clothing expenditures, savings needs) decrease after retirement. Also known as the *replacement ratio.*

incontestable clause   Life insurance policy clause that provides a time limit (usually two years) on the insurer's right to dispute a policy's validity based on material misstatements made in the application. Also known as an *incontestability provision.* See also *contestable period.*

increasing term insurance   A type of term insurance in which the death benefit of the policy increases during the term of coverage. The death benefit may increase at stated intervals by some specified amount or percentage, or it may increase according to increases in the cost of living.

incurred but not reported (IBNR) claims   Claims that were incurred in an accounting period but that were not reported to the insurer as of the Annual Statement date.

incurred claim loss ratio   For a group insurance contract, the ratio of the claims incurred during a certain period to the premium earned by the insurance company during the same period. This ratio shows how much of the premium paid for a policy is used to cover claims paid and accrued.

indemnity   See *contract of indemnity.*

indemnity benefits   Medical expense insurance plan benefits that are stated as a specified maximum dollar amount that will be reimbursed for each covered service. Also known as *reimbursement benefits.* Contrast with *service benefits.* Most commercial insurers previously provided indemnity benefits but many now provide service benefits.

independent life brokers   Licensed brokers who operate independently and specialize in selling particular types of products or meeting the business coverage or estate planning needs of certain target markets.

independent marketing organization (IMO)   A non-company affiliated organization that contracts with an insurance company to perform distribution and other marketing functions for one or more of the company's products or product lines.

independent property/casualty (P/C) brokers   Independent, multi- pleline agents or agencies that are primarily engaged in the distribution of property/casualty products and that make up what is commonly known in the property/casualty insurance industry as the independent agency system or the American Agency System.

indeterminate premium life insurance   A type of nonparticipating whole life insurance that specifies both a maximum potential premium rate and a lower premium rate. The lower rate is paid by the policyowner for a specified period (from 1 to 10 years) immediately after the policy is purchased. Later, the premium rate may fluctuate according to the mortality, expense, and investment experience of the insurance company, but the premium rate will never be larger than the maximum premium rate. Also called *flexible premium life insurance, nonguaranteed premium life insurance,* and *variable premium life insurance.*

indexation   In pension planning, the adjustment of postretirement benefits to compensate for the effects of inflation. Benefits are generally indexed to increase in accordance with an increase in the level of a price index, such as the Consumer Price Index (CPI). See also *cost-of-living adjustment (COLA).*

indexed life insurance   A whole life insurance policy in which the death benefit and, consequently, the premium rate of the policy varies each year according to changes in a prescribed price index, such as the Consumer Price Index (CPI).

individual account plan A pension plan funded according to a defined contribution formula. Each participant's benefits are based on the amount contained in that individual's account. See *defined contribution formula* and *defined contribution pension plan.*

individual cession administration In reinsurance, a system of administration whereby the ceding company sends a separate notification to the reinsurer for each individual cession, and the reinsurer prepares its own records of cessions. Also called *traditional cession administration.* See also *cession card.* Contrast to *self-administration.*

individual employer groups A group insurance market segment composed of single employers providing coverage for employees through a policy—the master contract—issued to the employer.

individual fraud A type of medical insurance fraud committed by individuals on their medical expense claims in order to obtain benefits in excess of their medical expenses. Contrast with *provider fraud.*

individual funding methods Pension plan funding methods in which the amount of contributions necessary to fund a plan is determined by first separately calculating the contributions for each of the plan's participants and then adding these amounts to arrive at the total required contribution for the plan. Contrast with *aggregate funding methods.*

individual insurance Insurance that is issued to insure the life or health of a named person or persons, rather than the life or health of the members of a group. Also called *ordinary insurance.* See also *ordinary life insurance.*

individual practice association (IPA) A means of organizing a health maintenance organization (HMO) in which the participating physicians maintain their own separate offices. Such physicians usually treat both private patients and HMO members. See also *group practice model (GPM).*

84

individual retirement account (IRA)   In the United States, a tax-sheltered savings plan that allows some citizens to make pre-tax contributions to an approved account. The contributions and investment earnings are taxable as income only when paid out. Investors can establish IRAs through a number of financial institutions, including insurance companies. See also *Keogh plan* and *simplified employee pension (SEP)*.

individual stop-loss coverage   A type of stop-loss insurance that provides benefits for each claim that exceeds a stated amount. Also known as *specific stop-loss coverage.*

industrial insurance   A form of life insurance which today accounts for a small percentage of the business sold through the home service distribution system but a considerable percentage of the insurance in force. It is characterized by (a) death benefits of $2,000 or less, (b) a weekly, biweekly, or monthly premium payment schedule, (c) the collection of premiums at the policyowner's residence by an agent, and (d) minimum underwriting requirements. See also *home service distribution system.*

in-house brokerage agency   A department established by an exclusive-agent company and staffed by company-employed brokerage sales people whose primary function is to solicit distribution agreements with other companies offering products that the exclusive-agent company itself does not manufacture. The company's agents can then broker business with those companies through the in-house brokerage agency.

initial deductible   See *deductible.*

initial premium   The first premium payable for an insurance contract.

initial reserve   The reserve on a policy at the beginning of any given policy year. The initial reserve includes the net annual premium then due.

inside build-up   See *cash value.*

insolvency The inability of an insurer to meet its financial obligations on time.

insolvency clause In the United States, a clause contained in most reinsurance contracts and required by most states. The clause specifies that, if the ceding company becomes insolvent, the reinsurer must pay the ceding company or its liquidator all reinsurance that comes payable, without reduction, even if the ceding company or its liquidator has failed to pay all or a portion of any claim.

inspection receipt A receipt given to the applicant when the applicant receives a policy for inspection. This inspection receipt states that the insurance is not in effect and that there has been no delivery of the policy in the legal sense.

inspection report A report made by a consumer reporting agency concerning a proposed insured's lifestyle, occupation, and economic standing. An inspection report is considered an investigative consumer report, as defined by the Fair Credit Reporting Act. See also *investigative consumer report.*

installation The term used to include all the activities from the time a prospect decides to purchase a group insurance policy to the time the master contract and its individual certificates are issued.

installment certificate A certificate issued to the beneficiary of a life insurance policy that specifies the amount of each benefit payment and/or the period during which benefit payments will be made under a settlement option. An installment certificate also specifies whether a beneficiary is allowed to withdraw all or part of the funds during the payment period. See also *settlement agreement* and *settlement options.*

installment refund annuity A refund annuity under which the refund is payable in a series of periodic payments. See also *cash refund annuity.*

installment refund option A form of *life income option with refund* which specifies that any proceeds remaining after the death of the beneficiary will be paid in installments to the contingent payee. Contrast with the *cash refund option.*

insurability provision An insurance provision stipulating that, for a policy to become effective, the insured must still be insurable at the time of policy delivery according to the underwriting rules and practices of the company.

insurability statement A questionnaire that an insurer may ask an applicant to complete when a considerable amount of time has elapsed between the time the application is received and the time the policy is actually issued. The purpose of the insurability statement is to determine if any insurability factors have changed since the original application was completed. Insurability statements help protect insurers from post-issue antiselection. See also *antiselection.*

insurability type temporary insurance agreement An agreement issued in conjunction with a conditional premium receipt that provides temporary life insurance coverage as of the date specified in the agreement on the condition that the proposed insured is insurable. See also *conditional premium receipts* and *temporary insurance agreements.* Compare to *approval type temporary insurance agreement.*

insurable interest A condition in which the person applying for an insurance policy and the person who is to receive the policy benefit will suffer a genuine loss or detriment if the event insured against occurs. Without the presence of insurable interest, an insurance contract is not formed for a lawful purpose and, thus, is void from the start.

insurance A system of protection against loss in which a number of individuals agree to transfer risk by paying certain sums of money, called premiums. These premiums create a pool of money which guarantees that the individuals will be compensated for losses caused by events such as fire, accident, illness, or death.

insurance agent An insurance company representative who sells insurance. An insurance agent locates prospective insurance customers, determines the insurance needs of each customer, and assists the customer in applying for insurance. Typically, an insurance agent will deliver the policy when the application is approved, will collect the initial premium, and will provide customer service to policyowners. Also called an *agent,* a *field underwriter,* or a *life underwriter.* See also *broker, detached agent, general agent (GA), personal producing general agent (PPGA),* and *soliciting agent.*

Insurance Companies Act The primary federal law that governs insurance companies operating in Canada.

Insurance Regulatory Information System (IRIS) In the United States, an information system developed by the NAIC to help state regulatory agencies assess the financial stability of individual insurance companies by means of a series of ratios derived from the companies' statutory annual statements.

insurance trust A common form of trust, created during the lifetime of the person who creates the trust, that is funded by insurance policies on the life of the trust's creator or by the proceeds of such policies.

insured (1) In the United States and Quebec, a person whose life is insured by an insurance policy (for individual life insurance policies, called the *life insured* in the rest of Canada). (2) In the common law provinces of Canada, the owner of an individual life insurance policy (called the *policyowner* in the United States and the *policyholder* or *owner* in Quebec). (For the purposes of this glossary, we have used this term as it is used in the United States and Quebec, except in the definitions of purely Canadian terms, in which cases we have made it clear that we are using the term as it is used in Canada.)

insured funding A method of funding a pension plan in which the plan sponsor purchases annuity or life insurance contracts on behalf of each participant. The insurance company guarantees a certain benefit to each retiree. See also *group deferred annuity.*

insurer   The party in an insurance contract that promises to pay a benefit if a specified loss occurs. Usually an insurance company.

insurer-administered group insurance plan   A group insurance plan for which the insurer maintains the necessary plan records. See also *self-administered group insurance plan.*

integrated deductible   A type of deductible included in some major medical expense plans that can be satisfied by amounts paid by the insured under basic medical expense plans. Contrast with *corridor deductible.*

integrated dental plan   A dental plan which is part of a major medical policy.

integrated pension plan   A private pension plan in which the benefits or contributions are coordinated with the benefits or contributions of a government-sponsored pension plan.

intercompany comparison   A method designed to help managers control and evaluate operating expenses by comparing their agencies or companies with industry averages.

interest-adjusted cost   One figure calculated under the interest-adjusted net cost (IANC) method of comparing the costs of life insurance policies. The interest-adjusted cost represents the average annual cost of a policy and is calculated using premiums, dividends, and cash values. Also called the *surrender cost index (SCI).*

interest-adjusted net cost (IANC) method   A method of comparing the costs of life insurance policies. The IANC method weights dividends and cash values according to how far into the future the various amounts are payable. Under this method, three amounts are calculated: the interest-adjusted cost, the interest-adjusted payment, and the equivalent level annual dividend. Also known as the *surrender cost index (SCI) method.* See also *cost comparison methods.*

interest-adjusted payment One figure calculated under the interest-adjusted net cost method of comparing the costs of life insurance policies. The interest-adjusted payment represents the average annual payment for the policy and is calculated using only premiums and dividends. Also called the *net payment cost index.*

interest maintenance reserve (IMR) In United States statutory accounting, a liability account that absorbs an insurer's investment gains and losses on fixed-income securities caused by changes in interest rates. The IMR minimizes the effects of these gains and losses on the insurer's capital and surplus.

interest option A settlement option under which the insurer invests the proceeds of a life insurance policy and pays interest on these proceeds to the payee.

interest-rate resolution See *crediting-rate resolution.*

interest-sensitive insurance See *investment-sensitive insurance.*

interest-sensitive whole life insurance A type of whole life insurance in which premium rates and cash values vary according to the insurer's assumptions regarding mortality, investment, and expense factors. Each policyowner can decide whether he or she wants favorable changes in assumptions to result in a lower premium or a higher cash value for the policy. If changes in assumptions result in a higher premium than that paid when the policy was purchased, the policyowner may choose to lower the policy's death benefit and maintain the previous premium or pay the higher premium and maintain the original death benefit. As with indeterminate premium life insurance, interest-sensitive whole life insurance guarantees that the premium will not increase above the rate guaranteed when the policy was purchased. Also called *current assumption whole life insurance.*

interim insurance agreements See *temporary insurance agreements.*

internal replacement The surrender of one life insurance policy in order to buy another insurance policy that is issued by the same insurer.

interpleader In the United States, a procedure under which an insurance company that is unable to determine the proper recipient of policy proceeds pays those proceeds to a court, which decides the proper recipient. In Canada, the process is called *payment of insurance money into court.*

intracompany comparison A method designed to help a manager control and evaluate agency operating expenses by comparing one agency or function with other agencies or functions in the same company.

investigative consumer report As defined by the Fair Credit Reporting Act, a consumer report that uses interviews with persons who are associated with, or who have knowledge of, the consumer in question in order to solicit information regarding the consumer's character, lifestyle, or general reputation. See also *inspection report.*

investment department In a life and health insurance company, the department that examines the financial marketplace, recommends investment strategies to the company's finance committee, and manages the company's investments according to the policies established by the company's board of directors.

investment facility contract See *separate account contract.*

investment-sensitive insurance A general category of insurance products in which the death benefit and the cash value vary according to the insurer's investment earnings. In investment-sensitive insurance products, policyowners share a portion of the insurer's investment risk. The exact benefit amounts for these policies cannot be computed in advance, beyond any guaranteed minimums. The specific products that make up this category of insurance include variable annuities, variable life insurance, and variable universal life insurance. Also called *interest-sensitive insurance.*

investment year method (IYM)   An accounting method in which an insurer keeps records of the interest rates it earns annually on funds assigned each year to accounts within the general account. Also called the *new money method.* Compare to the *portfolio method.*

involuntary plan termination   The curtailment of a pension plan initiated by a government organization, such as the Pension Benefit Guaranty Corporation (PBGC) in the United States, rather than by the plan sponsor. Contrast with *voluntary plan termination.* See also *distress termination* and *standard plan termination.*

IPA   See *individual practice association (IPA).*

IPG contract   See *immediate participation guarantee (IPG) contract.*

IRA   See *individual retirement account (IRA).*

IRIS   See *Insurance Regulatory Information System (IRIS).*

irrevocable beneficiary   A beneficiary whose rights to the proceeds of a life insurance policy cannot be cancelled by the policyowner unless the beneficiary consents. Contrast with *revocable beneficiary.* See also *beneficiary.*

issue strain   See *surplus strain.*

issuing bank   A mutual savings bank that sells and issues life insurance policies in its own name. Each issuing bank issues its own contracts, keeps its own records, and invests the assets of its own insurance department. See also *agency bank* and *savings bank life insurance (SBLI).*

IYM   See *investment year method (IYM).*

jet screening   The process of evaluating simple applications for insurance as quickly as possible according to strictly defined underwriting criteria.

jet unit   An underwriting approach in which a group of entry-level or trainee underwriters screens some types of applications and approves those that meet certain well-defined criteria for acceptance. Also called a *speedy issue unit.*

JL&S   See *joint life and last survivor option (JL&S).*

joint and survivor annuity   An annuity whose income benefits are paid to two or more individuals until both or all of the individuals die. Also called a *joint and last survivorship annuity.*

joint and survivorship option   A life insurance settlement option under which payments will be made to two or more payees. These payments will continue until both or all the named payees are deceased.

joint credit life insurance   Credit life insurance that pays the full benefit amount to a lender upon the death of any of the cosigners of a loan.

joint life and last survivor option (JL&S)   In Canada, a pension plan provision that provides for the continuation of pension benefits to the spouse of a retired plan participant after the death of the participant. The survivor's benefits, which usually are not as large as the original benefits, continue until the death of the spouse. The provision is required in most Canadian jurisdictions, unless the participant (with spouse approval) elects to forego it. A very similar provision, called a *qualified joint and survivor (QJ&S) annuity,* is required in the United States for qualified pension plans.

joint mortgage redemption insurance   Decreasing term life insurance that covers the lives of two people who have taken out a mortgage. If one of the insureds dies, the insurer pays proceeds equal to the remaining amount owed on the mortgage to the beneficiary, who is usually the other insured. The beneficiary is not required to use the proceeds to pay off the mortgage. See also *mortgage redemption insurance.*

joint whole life insurance   One insurance policy that covers two lives and that provides for payment of the proceeds at the time of the first insured's death. Also called *first-to-die life insurance.*

jumbo limit In an automatic reinsurance treaty, the maximum dollar amount allowable of total insurance in force or applied for on an individual for a ceded risk to be automatically accepted by a reinsurer.

juvenile insurance policy An insurance policy purchased by an adult to cover the life of a child.

Keogh plan In the United States, an individual retirement account that a self-employed individual may establish and that benefits from favorable tax treatment.

key employee In pension planning in the United States, a highly paid employee who satisfies any one of four criteria relating to compensation and company ownership. The criteria are described in legislation and tax rules. The amount of benefits accrued to key employees in a pension plan, as compared to benefits accrued to other employees, is the major factor in determining whether the plan is a top-heavy employee benefit plan. See *top-heavy plan.*

key-person life insurance Life insurance purchased by a business on the life of a person (usually an employee) whose continued participation in the business is necessary to the firm's success and whose death or disability would cause financial loss to the company.

lapse The termination of an insurance policy because a renewal premium is not paid before the end of the grace period.

lapse rate For a block of policies, the percentage of in-force policies that terminate as a result of nonpayment of renewal premiums during a given policy year. The lapse rate is determined by dividing the number of policies that lapse during a given policy year by the number of policies in force at the beginning of that policy year. Also called the *voluntary termination rate* or *withdrawal rate.* Contrast with *persistency rate.*

large claim management See *case management.*

last survivor life insurance Whole life insurance that covers two persons and provides for payment of the proceeds when both insureds have died. It is generally designed to pay estate taxes. Also known as *second-to-die life insurance.*

late-remittance offer A means of encouraging reinstatement of lapsed insurance policies. A late-remittance offer specifies that the company will accept an overdue premium after the grace period ends and will reinstate the policy without requiring the policyowner to complete a reinstatement application or submit evidence of insurability. Also called a *late-payment offer.*

late retirement age Retirement after the normal retirement age (usually age 65) contained in a pension plan. In the United States, a qualified pension plan generally cannot force a plan participant to retire at the normal retirement age or any other age and generally cannot stop accruing pension benefits for a plan participant who elects to work beyond the normal retirement age. See also *early retirement age* and *normal retirement age.*

law of large numbers The theory of probability which specifies that the greater the number of observations made of a particular event, the more likely it will be that the observed results will approximate the results anticipated by the mathematics of probability.

layering In reinsurance, the practice of ceding risks in bands, called "layers." For example, the first $500,000 of a risk might be ceded to one reinsurer, the next $500,000 to another reinsurer, and so on.

lead reinsurer In a group or pool of reinsurers, a reinsurer that takes responsibility for underwriting and pricing risks which are submitted to the group for reinsurance on a facultative basis. The other members of the group agree to accept the underwriting and pricing decisions of the lead reinsurer and to share proportionately all the risks that are accepted for reinsurance.

ledger proposal A printed illustration of a policy's premium rates, cash values, and applicable dividends over a specified number of years.

legal actions provision   In an individual health insurance policy, a provision that limits the period during which a claimant may sue the insurer to collect a disputed claim amount.

legal reserve   See *statutory policy reserve.* See also *reserve* for a list of many different kinds of reserves.

legal reserve system   The modern system used to price life insurance in which the premium for each policy is directly related to the amount of risk the insurer assumes for that policy.

letters patent   In Canada, a procedure used by insurance companies wishing to incorporate through the federal government or in the provinces of Quebec, New Brunswick, Prince Edward Island, and Manitoba to petition the appropriate government agency for incorporation.

level commission schedule   A commission schedule that provides the same commission rate for the first and renewal years.

level premium annuity   A deferred annuity for which the purchaser of the annuity pays equal premium amounts at regular intervals, such as monthly or annually, until the date the benefit payments are scheduled to begin.

level premiums   Premiums that remain the same each year that the life insurance policy is in force.

level premium system   A life insurance pricing system whereby the purchaser pays the same premium amount each year the policy is in force.

level premium whole life insurance   A type of whole life insurance for which equal premiums are payable throughout the premium payment period.

level term insurance   A type of term insurance that provides a death benefit that remains the same during the term of coverage.

levelized commission schedule A commission schedule that provides different percentages for first-year and renewal commissions, but the differences between these percentages are smaller than the differences between first-year and renewal commissions under traditional commission schedules. Also known as a *heaped commission schedule.*

leveraged business See *minimum deposit business.*

leveraged ESOP An employee stock ownership plan (ESOP) that borrows money and uses the borrowed funds to buy stock of the employer. The employer then makes regular contributions to the plan on behalf of the participating employees. The ESOP uses this contributed money to pay back the loan and allocates the stock little by little to the employees. The employer's contributions are tax deductible for the employer and tax deferred for the employee.

liabilities A company's debts and future obligations. For an insurance company, liabilities include amounts owed to creditors and the actual and expected claims of its policyowners and their beneficiaries.

liability insurance A kind of insurance that provides a benefit payable on behalf of a covered party who is held legally responsible for harming others or their property.

licensed broker An insurance salesperson who is not under an agency contract with any insurance company, and who is usually considered to be an agent of the client rather than of the insurer. Also known as a *pure broker.*

LICTI See *life insurance company taxable income (LICTI).*

life annuity An annuity that provides periodic benefit payments for at least the lifetime of a named individual, called the annuitant.

life annuity with period certain A life annuity which promises that, if the annuitant dies before the end of a designated period (usually 5, 10, or 20 years), the insurer will continue payments to a contingent payee until the end of the designated period. Also called a *life income with period certain annuity.*

life income option A life insurance settlement option under which the insurer uses the policy proceeds and interest to pay the beneficiary a series of equal payments for as long as the beneficiary lives.

life income option with period certain A life insurance settlement option in which the insurer guarantees to pay the beneficiary a series of equal payments for a designated period, such as 10 years; thereafter, the payments will continue only as long as the original beneficiary lives. If the original beneficiary dies during the guaranteed period, payments will be made to a recipient designated by the original beneficiary until the end of the guaranteed period, at which time all payments will stop.

life income option with refund A type of life income settlement option in which the insurer guarantees that if the beneficiary dies before the total amount paid under the option equals the proceeds of the policy, then the insurer will pay the difference to a contingent payee. Also call a *refund life income option.* See also *cash refund option, installment refund option,* and *settlement options.*

life income with period certain annuity See *life annuity with period certain.*

life income with refund annuity An annuity that provides annuity benefits throughout the annuitant's lifetime and guarantees total benefit payments of at least the purchase price of the annuity. If the annuitant dies before the total benefit payments made equal the purchase price, the insurer pays a refund to the contingent payee equal to the difference between the purchase price and the amount that has been paid in benefits. See also *cash refund annuity* and *installment refund annuity.*

life insurance Insurance that provides protection against the economic loss caused by the death of the person insured.

life insurance company taxable income (LICTI) The difference between a life insurance company's gross income and its tax deductions.

life insurance policy A policy under which the insurance company promises to pay a benefit upon the death of the person who is insured.

life insured In the common law provinces of Canada, the person whose life is insured by an individual life insurance policy. Called the *insured* in the United States and Quebec. (For the purposes of this glossary, we have used the U.S. term "insured", except in definitions of purely Canadian terms. In those cases we have made it clear that "life insured" is a Canadian term.)

lifetime maximum For any individual, the maximum amount that a medical expense policy will pay for all the eligible medical expenses the individual incurs while insured under the policy.

life underwriter See *insurance agent.*

limited coverage policy See *dread disease coverage.*

limited-payment whole life insurance An insurance policy for which premiums are payable for some stated period that is less than the insured's lifetime. Some limited-payment policies specify the number of years during which premiums are payable, while other policies specify an age after which premiums are no longer payable. Single-premium whole life insurance, in which only one premium payment is made, is an extreme type of limited-payment insurance.

line In reinsurance, a way of referring to the dollar amount of the ceding company's retention on a risk or class of risk. Automatic reinsurance treaties are often expressed in terms of lines. For example, a two-line treaty is one in which the reinsurer agrees to reinsure automatically up to twice the amount of the ceding company's retention.

Linton yield method See *rate of return method.*

liquidation period See *payout period.*

living benefit rider See *accelerated death benefit rider.*

loading A charge that the insurer adds to the net premium to produce the gross premium actually paid by the policyowner. The loading covers the operating expenses of the company, to compensate the company for the loss of income when policies lapse, to provide contingency funds for unexpected events, and to provide margins for profits and contributions to surplus.

location-selling distribution system A system that distributes insurance products by locating insurance offices or kiosks in places where consumers generally shop for other items or take care of other business matters, such as department stores, grocery stores, and banks. Also known as the *retail outlet distribution system.*

lock-box banking A method of premium collection in which premium payments are received at a specified post office box. The insurer authorizes a bank to have access to that box and to remove and open the mail. All premium payments are deposited immediately in the bank, and the returned portions of the premium notices, along with a record of deposits, are sent to the insurer.

lock-in concept Under generally accepted accounting principles, a feature of reserve calculations which holds that, once an insurer adopts a set of reserve assumptions for a particular group of policies for a particular year of issue, these assumptions must continue prospectively; that is, they must be used for reserve calculations in future years.

long-form reinstatement application A reinstatement application similar to a policy application in that both address the long-term health history of the insured.

long-term care (LTC) benefit An accelerated death benefit provided by some individual life insurance policies under which the insurer agrees to pay a monthly benefit to an insured who requires constant care for a medical condition.

long-term care (LTC) insurance Coverage that provides medical and other services to insureds who need constant care in their own home or in a nursing home.

long-term disability income insurance In group insurance, disability income insurance whose maximum benefit period is greater than one year. The maximum benefit period commonly extends to retirement or age 70. In individual insurance, disability income insurance where maximum benefit period is greater than five years, commonly extending to age 65 or for the insured's lifetime. See also *disability income insurance* and *short-term disability income insurance.*

loss limit A factor used in the calculation of group life and health insurance dividends to minimize the effects of fluctuations in the amounts of claims from year to year. A loss limit is the maximum amount of claims that will be used in the calculation of dividends for any policy year.

loss of time insurance See *disability income insurance.*

loss rate The rate at which covered losses are expected to occur in a specified group of insureds.

loss ratio In pricing health insurance, the loss ratio is a means of comparing claims losses to premium earnings. To determine its loss ratio, an insurer divides the dollar amount of claims paid by the dollar amount of premiums received.

LTC benefit See *long-term care (LTC) benefit.*

LTC insurance See *long-term care (LTC) insurance.*

maintenance expenses The costs of keeping a policy in force. Maintenance expenses include the cost of processing premium payments and making policy dividend payments and the time that agents and customer service personnel spend in servicing and conserving policies that are in force.

major medical insurance A type of medical expense insurance that provides broad coverage for most of the expenses associated with treating a covered illness or injury. See also *comprehensive major medical insurance* and *supplemental major medical insurance.*

major services In dental insurance, services, such as inlays, crowns, prosthodontics, and orthodontics, which are often covered at 50 percent of their reasonable and customary charges.

managed care A method of integrating both the financing and delivery of health care within a system that seeks to manage the cost, accessibility, and quality of care.

managing general agent (MGA) An independent contractor who is authorized to appoint PPGAs on a company's behalf and who may represent more than one company.

mandatary In Quebec, a party who is authorized by another party, the mandator, to act on the mandator's behalf in contractual dealings with third parties.

mandated benefit A benefit required by state law to be included in a health insurance policy.

mandator In Quebec, a party who authorizes another party, the mandatary, to act on the mandator's behalf in contractual dealings with third parties.

manual An insurer's book of rates for use in setting premiums.

manual rating A method of setting group insurance premium rates under which, rather than using the group's past claims experience, the insurer uses its own past experience—and sometimes the experience of other insurers—to estimate the group's expected claims and expense experience. Manual rates are often used to establish premium rates for groups with no credible loss experience, such as small groups and groups that have not previously been insured. See also *blended rates* and *experience rating.*

MAP (Monitoring Attitudes of the Public) Survey Provided by the American Council of Life Insurance (ACLI), a survey which uses in-depth interviews with representative samples of the adult U.S. population to provide the industry with information on consumers' changing viewpoints toward life and health insurance products, insurance agents, the insurance industry, and other aspects of the marketing environment.

marketing committee In an insurance company, an interdepartmental committee that makes recommendations on the design of insurance contracts, specific coverages to be provided under these contracts, premium rates, and guarantees to be included in contracts.

marketing department The department in an insurance company responsible for getting insurance products to the company's customers. The marketing department normally conducts market research, works with other departments in the company to develop new products and revise current ones to meet the needs of the company's customers, prepares advertising campaigns (in conjunction with the company's executive office and corporate communications committee), designs promotional materials, and establishes and maintains distribution systems for the company's products.

master contract The legal contract between an insurance company and a group insurance policyholder. The master contract insures a number of people under a single contract. Also called the *master policy.* See also *certificate of insurance.*

master plan A standardized form of pension or other employee-benefit plan developed by a financial institution to simplify plan drafting for plan sponsors. Although similar to a prototype plan, a master plan usually refers to a plan document developed by a financial institution (like an insurer) that can be adopted only by plan sponsors who use that financial institution to fund the plan.

master policy See *master contract.*

matching contributions In the United States, contributions made by an employer to an employee's Section 401(k) plan (cash or deferred arrangement) and designed to equal the employee's contributions up to a certain amount or percentage of compensation. See also *elective contributions* and *nonelective contributions.*

material fact   A fact that is relevant to an insurance company's underwriting decision regarding issuing or rating a policy.

material misrepresentation   In insurance, a misstatement by an applicant that is relevant to the insurer's acceptance of the risk, because, if the truth had been known, the insurer would not have issued the policy or would have issued the policy on a different basis.

matured endowment   An endowment insurance policy that has reached the end of its term during the lifetime of the insured and is therefore payable.

maturity date   (1) The date on which an endowment insurance policy's face amount will be paid to the policyowner if the insured is still living. (2) The date on which an insurer begins to pay periodic benefits under an annuity. Also known as the *annuity date.*

maximum benefit   The largest benefit amount that a defined benefit pension plan is legally permitted to provide to a plan participant. In the United States, the maximum benefit is determined under Section 415 of the Internal Revenue Code. The maximum benefit is subject to legislative change and is generally indexed to inflation so that it increases as price levels increase. In Canada, a maximum pension benefit is also established under taxation rules. See also *contribution limit* and *Section 415 limits.*

maximum benefit period   The maximum length of time for which disability income payments will continue.

maximum benefits for related confinements provision   A provision included in basic hospital and surgical policies that limits the maximum benefits for all hospital confinements and for all surgery performed during one period of sickness or for any single injury.

McCarran-Ferguson Act A law enacted by the U.S. Congress allowing states to regulate the insurance industry, as long as state regulation is deemed to be adequate. Also known as Public Law 15.

MCCSR See *Minimum Continuing Capital and Surplus Requirements (MCCSR).*

MDO insurance See *monthly debit ordinary (MDO) insurance.*

mean reserve The average of the initial reserve and the terminal reserve of a life insurance policy in any given policy year.

Medicaid A government-funded program in the United States that provides medical expense coverage for eligible people under age 65 who are indigent and meet certain other criteria. The program is administered by the states and is supported by state and federal funds.

medical application An application for insurance in which the proposed insured is required to undergo some type of medical examination. The results of the medical examination are then reported to the insurance company.

medical case management See *case management.*

medical expense insurance Any of several types of health insurance designed to pay for part or all of an insured's health care expenses, such as hospital room and board, surgeon's fees, visits to doctors' offices, prescribed drugs, treatments, and nursing care. See also *basic medical expense coverage, major medical insurance,* and *specified expense coverage.*

Medical Information Bureau (MIB) An organization that serves as a clearinghouse for medical information for the life insurance industry. When a person applies for life insurance, the insurance company sends the applicant's medical test results and any indication of health impairments to the MIB. This information is then available to other insurers when they are investigating an applicant's insurability.

Access to MIB-coded information is restricted to authorized medical, underwriting, and claim personnel in member companies. No member company can request information from the MIB unless the individual being investigated gives written consent. An insurance company cannot base its underwriting decision solely on information provided by the MIB.

medical necessity provision A condition included in most major medical expense plans, stating that medical services that are educational or experimental in nature are not eligible for coverage.

medical report A report on a proposed insured's health that is completed by a physician and is based on a physical examination and questioning of the proposed insured. Such a medical report serves as part of a medical application.

Medicare A United States government program that provides medical expense coverage to persons age 65 and over and to people with certain disabilities, as specified by Congress.

Medicare carve-out Medical expense coverage offered by employers to retired employees that reduces medical expense benefits to the extent that those benefits are provided by Medicare.

Medicare supplement Medical expense coverage that provides benefits for certain expenses not covered under Medicare. This coverage is available only to individuals who are covered by Medicare and can be purchased by individuals or by employers to cover retired employees.

member contribution See *percentage contribution.*

memorandum of association In Canada, a document of incorporation that can be used by insurance companies wishing to incorporate in the provinces of British Columbia, Alberta, Saskatchewan, Ontario, Newfoundland, or Nova Scotia. This document contains the fundamental terms for registering for incorporation.

MEWA See *multiple-employee welfare agreement (MEWA).*

MGA See *managing general agent (MGA)*.

MIB See *Medical Information Bureau (MIB)*.

midterminal reserve The average of a health insurance policy's terminal reserve for the previous policy year and the terminal reserve for the current policy year.

minimum age requirement In pension planning, a requirement that an employee attain a certain age before being permitted to participate in the employer's pension plan. In the United States, a private employer's qualified pension plan cannot have a minimum age requirement greater than age 21. See also *minimum service requirement*.

minimum cession In an automatic reinsurance treaty, the smallest amount that a reinsurer will reinsure for any particular policy. See also *corridor*.

Minimum Continuing Capital and Surplus Requirements (MCCSR) A requirement that Canadian insurers maintain at least a minimum level of capital and surplus that reflects the riskiness of their assets and operations.

minimum deposit arrangement An arrangement whereby a policyowner can apply the first-year cash value of a policy to the initial premium amount.

minimum deposit business The use of policy loans to pay premiums. In minimum deposit business, a policyowner instructs the insurance company to pay the premium out of the policy's cash value and to bill the policyowner for a premium only if the cash value is insufficient to pay the premium. Also called *leveraged business*.

minimum funding standard account See *funding standard account*.

minimum funding standards In the United States, standards established under Section 412 of the Internal Revenue Code relating to the advance funding of qualified pension plans. The standards are designed to ensure that contributions to a qualified plan are adequate to meet the plan's current and future obligations. Failure to satisfy minimum funding standards can lead to penalty taxes and enforcement actions. See also *funding standard account.*

minimum premium plan (MPP) A group health insurance plan that is partially self-insured by the group policyholder but fully administered by an insurance company. The group policyholder provides the funds to pay claims up to a total specified amount; thereafter, the insurer pays claims from its own funds. See also *administrative services only (ASO) contract* and *self-insured group insurance plan.*

minimum reserve requirements In the United States, guidelines required under the Standard Valuation Law for insurers to apply in calculating statutory policy reserves. The minimum reserve requirements specify the mortality tables, interest rates, and other factors that must be used to calculate the minimum values of an insurer's policy reserves. An insurer can use policy reserves that are greater than those calculated using the minimum reserve requirements, but not reserves that are smaller.

minimum service requirement In pension planning, a requirement that an employee complete a certain period of employment (often known as a probationary or waiting period) before being permitted to participate in the employer's pension plan. In the United States, an employee who meets minimum age requirements generally cannot be subject to a waiting period of more than one year, although a plan with full and immediate vesting of benefits can require a two-year waiting period. In Canada, a two-year waiting period is permissible. See also *minimum age requirement.*

misrepresentation (1) A false or misleading statement made to induce a prospect to purchase insurance. Misrepresentation is a prohibited insurance sales practice. (2) A false or misleading statement made by an applicant for insurance. Certain misrepresentations provide a basis for the insurer to avoid the policy.

misstatement of age or sex provision A provision that is typically included in life insurance and annuity policies and that describes how the amount of the policy benefit will be adjusted if the age or sex of the insured or the annuitant is incorrectly stated.

mixed model HMO An HMO that combines certain characteristics of two or more of the various types of HMO models.

MLA system See *multiple-line agency (MLA) system.*

modco See *modified coinsurance (modco) plan.*

mode of premium payment The frequency with which premiums are paid (for example, annually, quarterly, monthly).

model bill Sample legislation developed by the National Association of Insurance Commissioners (NAIC) in the United States or the Canadian Council of Insurance Regulators (CCIR) in Canada to encourage uniformity of state or provincial regulation. States and provinces may adopt this sample legislation exactly as written or use it as the basis for developing their own laws.

Model Life Insurance Solicitation Regulation In the United States, a regulation adopted by the NAIC in 1976 that requires insurers to give life insurance consumers (1) information that will improve their ability to select the most appropriate plan of life insurance to meet their needs, (2) an understanding of the basic features of the policy that has been purchased or that is under consideration, and (3) the ability to evaluate the relative costs of similar plans of life insurance.

model office A mathematical model composed of a number of hypothetical situations, such as a company's total forecasted sales for a particular product at various combinations of issue ages and face amounts, that in total will reasonably reflect the entire range of the product's sales which will occur in real life.

Model Rules Governing the Advertisement of Life Insurance In the United States, an NAIC model law which provides a set of comprehensive guidelines covering nearly all aspects of advertisements for life insurance policies and annuity contracts.

Model Unfair Trade Practices Act   In the United States, an NAIC model law that prohibits unfair trade practices, such as defamation, rebating, unfair discrimination, and unfair claim settlement practices; the law contains a general prohibition against any form of insurance advertising that is "untrue, deceptive, or misleading."

modified coinsurance (modco) plan   A plan of reinsurance in which the basic provisions of coinsurance are modified by having the ceding company maintain the entire policy reserve. At the end of each year, the reinsurer transfers back to the ceding company an amount equal to the increase in the reserve for the reinsured portion of the policy less the interest earned by the ceding company on the reserve for the reinsured portion of the policy. In the event of a claim, the reinsurer is responsible for the death benefit of the reinsured portion of the policy less the reserve credited for that amount.

modified net premiums   Net premiums that are other than level, generally being lower for the first year than for subsequent years.

modified-premium whole life insurance   A type of whole life insurance in which the policyowner pays a lower than normal premium for a specified initial period, such as five years. After the initial period, the premium increases to a stated amount that is somewhat higher than usual. This higher premium is then payable for the life of the policy.

modified reserve method   In the United States, a method for calculating policy reserves that creates smaller first-year statutory reserves than those calculated using the net level premium approach. Modified reserve methods reduce surplus strain. The most common modified reserve method is the full preliminary term method. See also *full preliminary term method, net level premium approach,* and *surplus strain.*

money market fund   A low-risk mutual fund that achieves great liquidity by investing primarily in short-term securities.

money-purchase pension plan A type of defined contribution plan that specifies a rate of contribution to each participant's account (for example, 8 percent of annual compensation) and results in a benefit that is equal to the amount in the participant's account (including investment gains and losses) at retirement. Upon retirement, the money that the employer has contributed, plus investment earnings, is often used to purchase an annuity which will provide a regular pension benefit.

Monitoring Attitudes of the Public Survey See *MAP (Monitoring Attitudes of the Public) Survey.*

monthly debit ordinary (MDO) insurance Whole life insurance that is marketed under the home service system and paid for by monthly premium payments, usually made to an agent. See also *home service distribution system.*

monthly outstanding balance method In group creditor insurance, a premium-paying arrangement for contributory plans whereby, every month, the lender adds to the outstanding balance of the loan an amount sufficient to insure that balance for one month. Contrast with *single-premium method.*

moral hazard The danger that a proposed insured might deliberately attempt to conceal or misrepresent information. Moral hazard is a risk factor that affects the underwriting decision. Compare to *physical hazard.*

morbidity Sickness, injury, or failure of health.

morbidity rate The rate at which sickness, injury, and failure of health occur among a defined group of people. The premium that a person pays for health insurance is based in part on the morbidity rate for that person's age group.

morbidity table A chart that shows the rates of sickness and injury occurring among given groups of people categorized by age.

mortality charge   The cost of the insurance protection element of a universal life policy. This cost is based on the net amount at risk under the policy, the insured's risk classification at the time of policy purchase, and the insured's current age.

mortality curve   A line graph that represents the mortality rates as they change from age to age.

mortality experience   The actual number of deaths occurring in a given group of people. Contrast with *expected mortality.*

mortality rate   The frequency with which death occurs or is expected to occur among a defined group of people.

mortality table   A chart that displays the incidence of death among a given group of people categorized by age. See also *aggregate mortality table, annuity mortality table, basic mortality table, select and ultimate mortality table, select mortality table, ultimate mortality table,* and *valuation mortality table.*

mortgage redemption insurance   Decreasing term life insurance that provides a death benefit amount corresponding to the decreasing amount owed on a mortgage. The beneficiary is not required to use the death benefit to pay off the mortgage. See also *joint mortgage redemption insurance.*

movement of securities return   A semiannual statement required of federally licensed insurers in Canada. The statement details transactions involving securities and loans made during the previous six months.

MPP   See *minimum premium plan (MPP).*

multi-company representation   In Canada, an arrangement by which a life and health insurance agent is allowed to represent more than one insurance company.

multi-employer plan A pension or other employee-benefit plan involving more than one employer and established by collective bargaining (negotiation between a union and employers). Coverage under the plan is portable within the group, which means that an employee who leaves one employer who is a member of the group and goes to work for another member of the group may continue coverage under the plan.

multiple-employer welfare agreement (MEWA) (1) An arrangement whereby several employers (often in the same industry) cooperate to procure group insurance for their employees. (2) An arrangement made by an insurance company to cover several employers under one master policy, usually with specific benefit packages and limitations.

multiple-line agency (MLA) system A distribution system that uses commissioned sales agents to distribute life, health, annuity, and property/casualty products of a group of affiliated insurance companies. Also known as the *multiple-line exclusive agency system* or *all-lines exclusive agency system.*

mutual benefit method An early method of funding life insurance, formerly used by fraternal orders or guilds. Under the mutual benefit method, the promised death benefit was provided by charging participating members an equal amount after the death of an insured member. Also called the *post-death assessment method.* See also *assessment method.*

mutual insurance company An insurance company owned by its policyowners. Contrast with *stock insurance company.*

mutualization The process of converting a stock insurance company to a mutual insurance company.

NAIC See *National Association of Insurance Commissioners (NAIC).*

NAIC Model Privacy Act A model bill written by the National Association of Insurance Commissioners and designed to set standards for the collection, use, and disclosure of information gathered for or by insurance institutions, agents, or insurance-support organizations.

NASD See *National Association of Securities Dealers (NASD).*

National Association of Insurance Commissioners (NAIC) In the United States, an association of state insurance commissioners designed to promote consistent insurance regulation. Although the NAIC has no legal power, the recommendations of the NAIC and the actions taken at its semiannual meetings carry great weight with the individual state insurance commissioners, the state legislatures, and the insurance industry. Similar to the *Canadian Council of Insurance Regulators (CCIR)* in Canada.

National Association of Securities Dealers (NASD) A voluntary association of securities firms empowered by the Maloney Act of 1938 to regulate the affairs of securities firms and to promote fair and ethical practices in the securities business.

national brokerage houses Large, independent firms that specialize in providing risk management and employee benefits advice to large, commercial clients.

National Organization of Life and Health Guaranty Associations (NOLHGA) In the United States, an organization supported by the individual state guaranty associations which are its members. It serves as a central source of information for the state associations and helps resolve problems created by the insolvency of insurers that are licensed in more than one state. See also *guaranty association.*

NAV See *net asset value (NAV).*

needs analysis Part of the fact-finding stage in the personal selling process; the process of developing a detailed personal and financial picture of a prospect in order to evaluate his or her insurance needs.

negotiated trusteeship An agreement resulting from collective bargaining (a negotiation between a union and one or more employers). This agreement provides group insurance for the members of the union. Also called a *Taft-Hartley Trust*.

net amount at risk The difference between the face amount of a life insurance policy—other than a universal life policy—and the amount of the policy's reserve at the end of a given policy year. For universal life insurance policies, the net amount at risk varies depending on whether the policyowner selects an Option A or an Option B plan.

net asset value (NAV) The value or purchase price of a share of stock in a mutual fund.

net benefit premium Under generally accepted accounting principles (GAAP), the portion of the premium that funds the benefit reserve.

net cash value See *cash surrender value.*

net cost (1) In individual insurance, any one of several different figures used to indicate the cost of an insurance policy. (2) In group insurance, premiums less dividends.

net expense premium Under generally accepted accounting principles (GAAP), the portion of the premium that covers the expenses of maintaining and acquiring the policy. See *loading.*

net gain The total of an insurer's income minus the total of its expenses, benefit payments, federal income taxes, and policyholder dividends, if the difference is positive.

net level annual premiums Net premiums that stay the same each year during the premium-payment period. See also *level premiums* and *net premium.*

net level premium approach A method used by U.S. insurers to calculate life insurance policy reserves, which assumes that a policy's net premiums do not increase or decrease during the life of the policy. Contrast with *modified reserve method.*

net loss The total of an insurer's income minus the total of its expenses, benefit payments, federal income taxes, and policyholder dividends, if the difference is negative.

net payment cost index See *interest-adjusted payment.*

net policy proceeds See *policy proceeds.*

net premium The amount of money needed to provide life insurance benefits for a policy. The net premium is calculated by using only an assumed interest rate and a tabular mortality rate. No loading for expenses is added. The net premium equals a policy's gross premium minus the policy's loading. See also *gross premium, loading, tabular interest rate,* and *tabular mortality rate.*

net premium rates Life insurance premium rates that are based only on expected mortality rates and investment earnings.

net single premium The present value of the expected benefits of an insurance policy. The net single premium is the amount of money that would have to be collected at the time a policy is issued to assure that there will be enough money to pay the death benefit of the policy, assuming that interest is earned at the expected rate and that claims occur at the expected rate.

network model HMO A type of group model HMO that contracts with more than one group practice of physicians to provide services to HMO members.

new business department See *underwriting department.*

new business strain See *surplus strain.*

new money method See *investment year method (IYM).*

no-evidence limit In group insurance, the maximum amount for which an insurance company will insure an individual without first securing evidence of insurability. Also known as the *guaranteed issue limit.*

NOLHGA See *National Organization of Life and Health Guaranty Associations (NOLHGA).*

no-load fund A mutual fund in which the investor buys shares directly from the fund and no sales commissions are paid.

nonadmitted assets In the United States, assets that cannot be included on the *Assets* page of a life insurance company's Annual Statement.

nonadmitted reinsurer In the United States, a reinsurer that is not licensed to accept reinsurance in a given jurisdiction. Also called *unauthorized reinsurer.* Contrast to *admitted reinsurer.*

noncancellable and guaranteed renewable policy An individual health insurance policy that the insurer cannot terminate and for which the premiums cannot be raised. See also *cancellable policy, conditionally renewable policy, guaranteed renewable policy, noncancellable policy,* and *optionally renewable policy.*

noncancellable policy An individual health insurance policy for which the premium cannot be raised by the insurer and which must be renewed by the insurer until the insured reaches a specified age, provided premiums are paid when due. See also *cancellable policy, conditionally renewable policy, guaranteed renewable policy, noncancellable and guaranteed renewable policy,* and *optionally renewable policy.*

noncontributory group insurance A group insurance plan in which the insureds pay no portion of the premium for their insurance. The group policyholder pays the entire premium. If a group plan is noncontributory, the enrollment of group members is automatic; all eligible group members are covered. Contrast to *contributory group insurance.*

noncontributory plan A pension or employee-benefit plan in which contributions are made entirely by the plan sponsor. Contrast with *contributory plan.*

nonduplication of benefits provision A provision that coordinates the medical expense benefit payments between two insurance carriers, allowing the secondary carrier to pay the difference, if any, between the amount paid by the primary plan and the amount that would have been payable by the secondary plan had that plan been the primary plan.

nonelective contributions In the United States, contributions other than matching contributions made by an employer to an employee's Section 401(k) plan (cash or deferred arrangement). The contributions are made using employer funds and not through a reduction of the employee's salary. See also *elective contributions* and *matching contributions.*

nonexclusive territory Under the general agency system, a territory in which more than one general agent may represent the same insurer. Compare to *exclusive territory* and *overlapping territory.*

nonforfeiture factors Special values, similar to annual premiums, that some insurers use to calculate their policies' cash values. Each insurer calculates its own nonforfeiture factor. In the United States, the nonforfeiture factor can never be greater than the adjusted premiums required by the Standard Nonforfeiture Law.

nonforfeiture options The various ways in which a policyowner may apply the cash value of a life insurance policy if the policy lapses. See also *automatic nonforfeiture option, automatic premium loan (APL), cash surrender value option, extended term insurance option,* and *reduced paid-up insurance option.*

nonforfeiture values The benefits, as printed in a life insurance policy, that the insurer guarantees to the policyowner if the policyowner stops paying premiums. These amounts may be used in a variety of nonforfeiture options.

nonguaranteed premium life insurance See *indeterminate premium life insurance.*

noninsured pension fund A pension fund that is not funded by insurance contracts.

nonmedical application An application for insurance in which the proposed insured is not required to undergo a medical examination. However, a nonmedical application does contain questions that the proposed insured must answer about his or her health. See also *nonmedical supplement.*

nonmedical declaration See *nonmedical supplement.*

nonmedical supplement A report that describes the proposed insured's health history. A nonmedical supplement is completed by the agent based on information provided by the proposed insured and can serve as part of a nonmedical application. Also called a *nonmedical declaration.* See also *nonmedical application.*

nonpar policy See *nonparticipating policy.*

nonparticipating policy A life insurance policy for which the policyowner does not share in the insurer's surplus through policy dividends. Also called a *nonpar policy.*

nonproportional reinsurance A type of reinsurance plan in which the amount (proportion) of the risk to be carried by the ceding company and the amount (proportion) of the risk to be carried by the reinsurer are not known at the time the reinsurance treaty is made. For example, see *catastrophic reinsurance plan, excess reinsurance plan,* and *stop-loss reinsurance plan.*

nonqualified annuity A type of annuity in the United States funded with money that has already been taxed by the federal government in the year in which the funds are deposited.

nonqualified deferred-compensation plan In the United States, a retirement income plan that does not meet the requirements of the Internal Revenue Service (IRS) for qualified plans. Although such plans do not receive the tax advantages of qualified plans, they need not satisfy the restrictive plan design requirements that qualified plans must satisfy. Nonqualified plans are often used as a benefit for executives or highly compensated employees.

nonresident license   A license authorizing an agent who resides in another state to sell insurance in the licensing state.

nonretroactive disability benefits   A type of disability benefit that is payable only for the period of disability that follows an elimination period.

nonscheduled dental plan   A dental plan which pays benefits for procedures based on the dentist's actual charges, as long as the charges are usual, customary, and reasonable. See also *combination dental plan* and *scheduled dental plan.*

nonsmoker risk class   An underwriting risk class that includes people who are standard risks and who have not smoked cigarettes for a specified period of time, usually 12 months, before applying for insurance. People in the nonsmoker risk class pay lower than standard premiums.

nontrusteed plan   See *general asset group insurance plan.*

nonvested commission   A commission that is payable to an agent only if the agent still represents the company when the commission becomes due.

normal cost   The actuarially determined amount needed to fund for one plan year the retirement benefits of a pension plan participant or of a pension plan as a whole. A plan's normal cost is dependent on the actuarial funding method and assumptions used by the plan.

normal retirement age   The earliest age at which a participant in a pension plan can retire and receive the plan's specified benefit in full. Usually age 65. See also *early retirement age* and *late retirement age.*

notched option A method of integrating private pension plans with Canadian public pension plans. Under this option, a participant who retires before age 65 receives a greater benefit from the private plan until age 65 and a smaller benefit after 65, when the participant begins to receive public pension payments. When both the public and private plan benefits are considered, the participant receives the same combined benefit payment before and after age 65. However, this benefit payment is smaller than the payment the participant would have received had he or she waited until reaching age 65 before beginning to receive benefits. The notched benefit is designed so that the sponsor pays the same total benefit as it would have if the amount of the private benefit payments had been constant throughout. Compare to *bridging supplement.*

numerical rating system A method of classifying risks in which each medical and nonmedical factor is assigned a numerical value based on its expected impact on mortality. See also *credits and debits.*

OAS See *Old Age Security Act (OAS).*

OASDHI See *Old Age, Survivors, Disability and Health Insurance Act (OASDHI)* and *Social Security.*

occupation class A group of occupations that present a similar risk to an insurance company. If all other factors are equal, people in the same occupation class will pay the same premium rates for health insurance.

Office of the Superintendent of Financial Institutions (OSFI) In Canada, the government office that administers the federal laws pertaining to the various financial institutions, including insurance companies.

offset A tax law provision that allows an insurer to use the amount paid for one type of tax to reduce another aspect of the company's tax liability.

offset approach A way of integrating benefits from a private defined benefit pension plan with benefits from a government plan. The benefit payable from the private plan is reduced by a specified percentage of the benefit received from the government plan.

Old Age Security Act (OAS) Canadian federal legislation that provides a pension to virtually all citizens who are age 65 or older.

Old Age, Survivors, Disability and Health Insurance Act (OASDHI) The legislation that created Social Security in the United States. See *Social Security.*

open contract A type of insurance contract used by fraternal benefit societies. Under this type of contract, the society's charter, constitution, and bylaws become a part of the insurance contract, and any amendments to them automatically become amendments to the insurance contract. No such amendment, however, can destroy or diminish benefits that the society is contractually obligated to pay. See also *closed contract* and *fraternal benefit society.*

open debit In a home service sales territory, a block of policyowners that does not have an assigned servicing agent.

open-ended HMO An HMO that provides benefits for medical care obtained from providers who do not belong to the HMO's network of providers, though usually at reduced benefit levels. Also known as a *point of service (POS) plan.*

open-panel HMO A type of HMO that allows any physician or health care provider who meets the HMO's specific standards to contract with the HMO to provide services to HMO members.

option A choice that a policyowner can make when deciding how to apply settlements, dividends, or nonforfeiture values. See also *dividend options, nonforfeiture options,* and *settlement options.*

option A plan A plan used in universal life insurance in which the potential policy proceeds remain level. In an option A plan, the policy proceeds are equal to the policy's death benefit. Consequently, the net amount at risk is equal to the difference between the policy's death benefit and the policy's cash value. As the cash value increases, the net amount at risk decreases. Contrast to *option B plan*.

option B plan   A plan used in universal life insurance in which the potential policy proceeds increase. In an option B plan, the policy proceeds are equal to the death benefit plus the policy's cash value. Consequently, the net amount at risk is always equal to the death benefit of the policy. Contrast to *option A plan*.

optional insured rider   See *second insured rider.*

optional modes of settlement   See *settlement options.*

optionally renewable policy   An individual health insurance policy that grants the insurer the right to refuse to renew the policy on certain dates specified in the policy. The insurer also may add coverage limitations to the policy and may increase the premium rate for a class of optionally renewable policies. See also *cancellable policy, conditionally renewable policy, guaranteed renewable policy, noncancellable and guaranteed renewable policy*, and *noncancellable policy.*

ordinary agency system   See *agency system.*

ordinary annuity   See *annuity immediate.*

ordinary insurance   See *individual insurance.*

ordinary life insurance   Life insurance which is available to individuals in relatively unrestricted maximum death benefit amounts, and premiums may be paid monthly or less frequently.

original age conversion   The conversion of a term life insurance policy to a whole life policy at a premium rate based on the age of the insured at the time the term policy was purchased.

orphan A policy for which the insurance agent who sold the policy is no longer available to provide customer service.

OSFI See *Office of the Superintendent of Financial Institutions (OSFI).*

outliers Medicare patients whose illnesses are unique and whose conditions may not be classifiable under one of the diagnostic related groups.

out-of-pocket maximum A limit on the amount of medical expenses that a group member must pay out of his or her own pocket.

outstanding premium In Canada, a premium that is due on or before the policy statement date but that has not been received by that date.

overinsurance An amount of insurance that is excessive in relation to the loss insured against.

overinsurance provision A provision in an individual health insurance policy specifying that, under certain circumstances, policy benefits will be reduced if the insured has more insurance than needed to cover medical expenses or if disability income would exceed the insured's predisability earnings. See also *coordination of benefits (COB) clause.*

overinsured person A person who is entitled to receive (1) more in benefits from his medical expense policies than the actual costs incurred for treatment or (2) disability income benefits that exceed the amount of his predisability earnings.

overlapping territory Under the general agency system, a territory in which some portion of the territory is open to an agent other than the general agent, while the rest of the territory is the exclusive domain of the general agent. See also *exclusive territory* and *nonexclusive territory.*

overlined See *over-retained.*

over-retained The situation in which an insurance or reinsurance company has accepted an amount of insurance which exceeds the company's normal capacity on a specific risk. Also referred to as *overlined.*

override See *overriding commission.*

overriding commission A commission earned by a field office manager that is based on the business produced by the agents in that office. An overriding commission may be earned each time an agent sells business or it may be based on the overall production of the field office. Also called the *override.*

PAC See *preauthorized check (PAC) system or prescribed annuity contract (PAC).*

package selling The process of putting a simple insurance plan into a standardized presentation and looking for prospects who can use that package of coverage.

paid-up additional insurance dividend option The dividend option under which the insurer uses each policy dividend to purchase paid-up additional insurance on the insured's life.

paid-up additions Additional life insurance purchased with policy dividends. No additional premiums are needed for paid-up additions. Also called *dividend additions.*

paid-up additions option benefit A supplementary benefit that allows the owner of a whole life insurance policy to purchase single-premium paid-up additions to the policy on stated dates in the future.

paid-up policy An insurance policy that requires no further premium payments.

paramedical report A report based on a physical examination and a medical history completed by a medical technician, a physician's assistant, or a nurse, rather than a physician. A paramedical report describes the health of a proposed insured and can serve as part of an insurance application.

par policy See *participating policy.*

partial disability A disability that prevents an insured from engaging in some of the duties of his or her usual occupation or from engaging in the occupation on a full-time basis.

partial disability benefit A flat amount specified in a disability income insurance policy that is payable when the insured suffers a partial disability. Usually the partial disability benefit is half the full disability benefit. See also *residual disability benefit.*

partial plan termination The termination of a pension or employee-benefit plan for one group of participants but not for another. Sponsors sometimes do this to reclaim some of the assets of an overfunded plan.

partial surrender provision See *withdrawal provision.*

participating policy An insurance policy under which the policyowner shares in the insurance company's divisible surplus by receiving policy dividends. Also known as a *par policy.* See also *dividend.*

participation limit (1) In reinsurance, an amount which the total insurance in force or applied for on any individual must not exceed or the reinsurer will decline to participate in any further coverage on that individual. The participation limit includes coverage with all insurers and, in many companies, applies primarily to accidental death benefit coverage. (2) See *relation of earnings to insurance clause.*

partnership insurance A type of business insurance designed to provide funds so the remaining partners in a business can buy the business interest of a deceased or disabled partner. See also *business-continu-ation insurance.*

past service The period of employment service rendered by an employee before a pension plan was begun or amended or before the employee enrolled in the pension plan. A plan sponsor must decide whether pension benefits will be credited to an employee for the employee's past service or only for current and future service. See also *future service.*

PAT See *preadmission testing (PAT).*

payee (1) The person or party who is to receive the proceeds of a life insurance policy in accordance with the terms of a settlement agreement. (2) The person who receives the periodic benefit payments during an annuity's payout period. See also *annuitant.*

payment of insurance money into court In the common law jurisdiction of Canada, an action that an insurer takes when the insurer admits liability to pay policy proceeds but cannot determine the proper recipient. Once the insurer pays the money into court, the insurer is discharged of any further liability under the policy. In Quebec, an insurer in such a situation can obtain a valid discharge of liability by paying the policy proceeds to the Minister of Finance. In the United States, the process is called *interpleader.*

payout option provision An annuity policy provision that lists and describes each of the payout options available to the contractholder.

payout period The period during which annuity benefit payments are made. Also known as the *liquidation period.*

payroll deduction plan (1) See *salary-reduction plan.* (2) A premium payment method under which an individual's employer deducts the employee's premium amount from his or her paycheck.

PBGC See *Pension Benefits Guaranty Corporation. (PBGC).*

PBSA See *Pension Benefits Standards Act (PBSA).*

PCP See *primary care physician (PCP).*

peer review group A local physicians' group that helps solve insurance claim disputes and promotes fair and ethical practices in the health-care industry.

pension A lifetime monthly income paid to a person who has retired.

Pension Benefits Acts Federal and provincial laws that govern the terms and operation of private pension plans in Canada.

Pension Benefit Guaranty Corporation (PBGC) In the United States, the organization that insures benefits in defined benefit pension plans. Its purpose is to make sure that all participants in qualified defined benefit pension plans receive the vested benefits to which they are entitled, even if their pension fund goes bankrupt.

Pension Benefits Guarantee Fund In Canada, a fund established in the province of Ontario to guarantee payment of benefits in the case of the insolvency of a defined benefit pension plan.

Pension Benefits Standards Act (PBSA) In Canada, federal legislation that governs the administration of pension plans covering federal employees and those individuals whose employment falls under the legislative authority of the Canadian Parliament (including workers in the transportation, telecommunications, and banking industries).

pension fund (1) The assets used to pay the pensions of retirees. (2) An investment institution established to manage the assets used to pay the pensions of retirees.

Pension Index In Canada, the index used by the Canada Pension Plan and Quebec Pension Plan to vary pension benefit payments to reflect the effects of inflation. The Pension Index is based on the Consumer Price Index (CPI).

pension plan An agreement under which an employer establishes a plan to provide its employees with a lifetime monthly income benefit that begins at their retirement.

pension trust See *trusteed pension plan.*

per capita beneficiary designation A class beneficiary designation under which life insurance policy proceeds are shared only by those class members who survive the insured. Contrast to *per stirpes beneficiary designation.*

per stirpes beneficiary designation A class beneficiary designation under which the descendants of a deceased class member receive the deceased class member's share of the life insurance policy proceeds. Contrast to *per capita beneficiary designation.*

per-cause deductible A deductible that must be satisfied for each separate accident or illness before major medical benefits will be paid. Also known as a *per-disability deductible.* Contrast with *all-causes deductible.*

per-cause maximum For any individual, the maximum amount that a medical expense policy will pay for medical expenses resulting from any particular illness or injury.

per-disability deductible See *per-cause deductible.*

percentage contribution The amount of the premium that a group member pays in a contributory group insurance plan. Also known as *employee contribution* or *member contribution.* See also *contributory group insurance.*

percentage participation See *coinsurance.*

per-disability deductible See *per-cause deductible.*

period certain A specified time during which an insurer unconditionally guarantees that benefit payments will continue under a settlement option or annuity.

permanent and total disability A condition that prevents an insured from returning to any gainful employment.

permanent life insurance Life insurance that provides coverage throughout the insured's lifetime and also provides a savings element that builds a cash value. For descriptions of traditional permanent (whole) life products see *continuous-premium whole life insurance,* *graded-premium whole life insurance, joint whole life insurance policy, limited-payment whole life insurance, modified-premium whole life insurance,* and *single-premium whole life insurance.* For descriptions of nontraditional whole life products see *adjustable life insurance policy, current assumption whole life insurance, indeterminate premium life insurance, universal life insurance, variable life insurance,* and *variable universal life insurance.*

persistency   The retention of business that occurs when a policy remains in force as a result of the continued payment of the policy's renewal premiums.

persistency bonuses   (1) Financial incentives given to agents and agency managers to reward good persistency results. (2) A bonus paid to a customer after a policy remains in force for a specified number of years.

persistency fee   See *service fee.*

persistency rate   For a block of policies, the share of business that remains in force during a specified period. Calculated as the ratio of the policies in force for which renewal premiums were paid during a given period to the policies for which premiums were due during that period. The persistency rate is the complement of the lapse rate. Contrast with *lapse rate.*

personal interview report   A report that contains the same types of information as an inspection report, except that the personal interview report relies on the proposed insured as the only source of information. See also *inspection report.*

personal producing general agency (PPGA) system   An insurance distribution system that uses PPGAs.

personal producing general agent (PPGA)   A commissioned insurance sales agent who generally works alone and engages primarily in prospecting and sales. A PPGA's contract generally resembles that of a general agent, but PPGAs are generally under contract to several insurance companies. Most PPGAs must meet minimum production requirements in order to maintain their contract with an insurer.

personal selling distribution system An insurance distribution system in which commissioned or salaried salespeople sell products by making face-to-face presentations to prospective purchasers.

physical examination provision A health insurance policy provision that grants the insurer the right to have an insured, who has submitted a claim, examined by a doctor of the insurer's choice at the insurer's expense.

physical hazard A physical characteristic that may increase the likelihood of loss. Compare to *moral hazard.*

placement ratio In facultative reinsurance, the number of risks ceded by a particular ceding company to a particular reinsurer divided by the number of risks submitted by that ceding company to that reinsurer for evaluation.

plan administrator (1) The person who is responsible for ensuring that a welfare benefit plan complies with ERISA's disclosure and reporting requirements. (2) The individual who is responsible for many aspects of the operation of a group retirement plan.

plan document A written document that is adopted by an employer and that specifies the terms of a pension plan.

plan participant An employee or union member covered by a private retirement plan established by an employer or union.

plan sponsor An entity that establishes and maintains a pension or employee-benefit plan. The plan sponsor is often an employer, but may be a union, a trade or professional association, or a committee composed of representatives of a number of employers or associations.

plan valuation See *actuarial valuation.*

point of sale underwriting See *immediate underwriting.*

point of service (POS) plan See *open-ended HMO.*

policy A written document that contains the terms of the contractual agreement between an insurance company and policyowner.

policy acquisition costs Costs that are directly attributable to the production of new business. Also called *acquisition expenses.*

policy administration department See *customer service department.*

policy anniversary The anniversary of the date on which a policy was issued. Sometimes simply called the *anniversary.*

policy benefit See *benefit.*

policy dividend See *dividend.*

policy fee system A pricing system for unbundled products whereby the customer pays a flat amount—called the policy fee—plus a specific rate per $1,000 face amount.

policy filing The process of obtaining legal permission to sell an insurance product in a specific jurisdiction.

policyholder (1) The company or organization that owns a group insurance contract (called the *group policyholder* in Canada). The policyholder of a group insurance contract does not have the same ownership rights under the contract that a policyowner has under an individual contract. (2) In Quebec, the owner of an individual life insurance policy (called the *policyowner* in the United States and the *insured* in the rest of Canada). Also sometimes called the *owner* in Quebec. (3) Often used interchangeably with *policyowner.*

policy loan A loan that is made to a life insurance policyowner by an insurer. A policy loan is secured by a policy's cash value and cannot exceed the cash value. When the policy benefits are paid, the amount of any outstanding policy loan made against the policy is deducted from the benefits.

policy loan provision A policy provision that grants the owner of a life insurance policy the right to take a loan for up to the policy's net cash value less one year's interest on the loan.

policyowner The person or party who owns an individual insurance policy. The policyowner is not necessarily the person whose life is insured. The terms policyowner and policyholder are frequently used interchangeably.

policyowner dividend See *dividend.*

policyowner's equity See *cash value.*

policyowner service department See *customer service department.*

policy premium method (PPM) A reserve method for Canadian insurers that uses gross premiums instead of net premiums, using the following equation: *Policy Reserve = Present Value of Future Benefits – Present Value of Future Gross Premiums.*

policy proceeds The amount that the beneficiary actually receives from a life insurance policy after adjustments have been made to the basic death benefit for policy loans, dividends, paid-up additions, late premium payments, and supplementary benefit riders. Compare to *basic death benefit* and *death benefit.* Also called *net policy proceeds.*

policy prospectus A document that contains important information about a variable life insurance policy and that is required to be presented to a prospect for such a policy.

policy provisions The statements, following the face page of an insurance policy, that describe the operation of the insurance contract.

policy purchase rider See *guaranteed insurability (GI) rider.*

policy record An insurance company file that contains all the information about an insurance policy the insurer needs in order to administer the policy.

policy reserve (1) A liability account that identifies the amount of assets that, together with the future premiums to be received from in-force policies, are expected to be sufficient to pay future claims on those in-force policies. (2) The actual assets that guarantee that the insurer will have sufficient funds to pay future claims. See *reserve* for a list of reserves.

policy summary A document, often in the form of a computer printout, that contains certain legally required data regarding the specific policy being considered by an applicant.

policy year The 12-month period between a policy's anniversaries.

pool In pool reinsurance, a name for the group of reinsurers taking part in the reinsurance arrangement.

pooling In group insurance, the practice of underwriting a number of small groups as one large group.

pool reinsurance An arrangement in which (a) several insurance or reinsurance companies with similar underwriting policies and standards agree to accept reinsurance business from one another automatically within certain limits and (b) the cost of reinsurance is allocated proportionately to all members, based on the loss ratios experienced by the whole group.

portability (1) A pension plan participant's right to transfer (usually tax-free) pension credits that have accrued under a pension plan sponsored by one employer to a plan sponsored by another employer. (2) The right of a person covered under a group insurance plan to continue coverage after leaving the group.

portable coverage Group insurance coverage that can be continued by an insured employee who leaves the covered group.

portfolio (1) A group of investments managed or owned by an individual or organization. (2) All of the products offered by an insurance company.

portfolio method A method of accounting among insurers in which each customer or policyowner receives a rate of interest equal to the average rate of interest earned on the entire portfolio of assets in the insurer's general account. Compare to the *investment year method (IYM)*.

POS (point of service) plan See *open-ended HMO*.

post-death assessment method See *mutual benefit method*.

post-notice As required by the Fair Credit Reporting Act, a form that the insurer must send to an applicant in cases in which the insurer has made an adverse decision based on information contained in a report from a consumer reporting agency.

power of agency An agent's right to act for an insurer. The power of agency is established through agency contracts between an insurer and its agents.

PPGA See *personal producing general agent (PPGA)*.

PPM See *policy premium method (PPM)*.

PPO See *preferred provider organization (PPO)*.

preadmission certification A component of utilization review under which the utilization review organization determines whether an insured's proposed nonemergency hospital stay or some other type of care is most appropriate and what the length of an approved hospital stay may be.

preadmission testing (PAT) A cost-containment technique used by some medical expense insurance plans under which patients have diagnostic tests performed before surgery on an outpatient basis instead of on an inpatient basis.

pre-approach letter A direct mail prospecting tool designed to help an agent secure an interview with a prospect. Pre-approach letters (1) are directed to prospects to whom a specific appeal can be made, (2) describe a financial/insurance need or product, and (3) state that an agent will call to discuss the topic further.

preauthorization of benefits provision See *predetermination of benefits provision.*

preauthorized check (PAC) system An automatic premium payment technique whereby the policyowner authorizes the insurer to generate a check against the policyowner's bank account to pay each renewal premium.

precertification of benefits provision See *predetermination of benefits provision.*

pre-contract training A trial program that permits an individual to prepare to become an agent while continuing to work at his or her current job until offered a full-time agent contract.

pre-death assessment method See *assessment method.*

predetermination of benefits provision A provision often included in dental policies which specifies that when dental treatments are expected to exceed a stated level, such as $100, $150, or $200, the dentist should submit to the insurer the proposed treatment plan for the patient so that the insurer can determine the amount payable by the dental plan. Also known as a *preauthorization of benefits provision, precertification of benefits provision,* or *pretreatment review provision.*

pre-existing condition (1) For most individual health insurance, an injury that occurred or a sickness that first manifested itself before the policy was issued and that was not disclosed on the application. (2) For most group health insurance, a condition for which an individual received medical care during the three months immediately prior to the effective date of coverage.

pre-existing conditions provision A health insurance policy provision stating that until the insured has been covered under the policy for a certain period, the insurer will not pay benefits for any pre-existing condition.

preference beneficiary clause A life insurance policy provision which states that if no beneficiary is named, the insurer will pay the policy proceeds to the first living individual listed in the policy. The provision might list the "spouse of the insured," followed by the "children of the insured," etc. Also called a *succession beneficiary clause.*

preferred beneficiary In Canada, a class of beneficiaries applicable to policies issued before June 30, 1962, and consisting of the spouse, children, parents, and grandchildren of the insured. The policyowner can change the beneficiary of a policy from a preferred beneficiary to a beneficiary who is not a preferred beneficiary only with the consent of the preferred beneficiary.

preferred provider organization (PPO) A managed care organization that contracts with a selected group of health care providers to deliver medical services to a specific group of covered individuals.

preferred risk class The risk category that is composed of proposed insureds who present a significantly less-than-average likelihood of loss. Sometimes called the *superstandard risk class.*

preliminary inquiry form A type of application form used when there is a high probability that a policy either will not be issued or will be issued with such a high substandard rating that the policy premium will be unacceptable to the applicant. Using a preliminary inquiry form usually brings a quick response from the underwriting department. Also called a *trial application.*

premium   The payment, or one of a series of payments, required by the insurer to put an insurance policy in force and keep it in force.

premium deficiency reserve   A name sometimes used for a special reserve which an insurance company establishes when the gross premium for a policy is less than the net premium used to calculate the policy reserve.

premium-delay arrangement   In group insurance, an agreement between an insurer and a policyholder to lengthen a group insurance policy's grace period, on a permanent basis, usually by 30, 60, or 90 days. This arrangement allows the policyholder to use the deferred premium amounts for the length of time by which the grace period is extended. The arrangement is usually only granted to companies with excellent credit ratings. Also called *deferred premium arrangement.*

premium deposits   Amounts that are left on deposit with the insurer for the payment of future premiums.

premium payment mode   See *mode of premium payment.*

premium receipt   A receipt that the sales agent gives to an applicant for insurance in exchange for the initial premium payment and that provides a proposed insured with temporary insurance coverage while the application is being underwritten. See also *binding premium receipt* and *conditional premium receipt.*

premium receipt book   A book given to the policyowner when a home service agent makes a policy sale. The premium receipt book contains prenumbered receipts that are signed by the agent when the agent collects a premium.

premium reduction dividend option   A life insurance policy dividend option under which the insurer applies policy dividends toward the payment of renewal premiums.

premiums paid in advance A premium paid in one accounting period for insurance coverage that does not begin until the next period.

premium suspense account An account used by insurers to record transactions that are intended as premiums but which insurers cannot accept as revenue until a particular event occurs.

premium taxes Taxes levied on an insurer's premium income.

pre-need funeral insurance Whole life insurance that provides funds to pay for the insured's funeral and burial.

pre-notice As required by the Fair Credit Reporting Act, advance notice to an insurance applicant from an insurer that an investigative consumer report may be made on the applicant.

prepaid care Health care provided to a subscriber in a traditional HMO in exchange for the payment of a fixed, periodic fee.

preretirement survivor annuity A pension plan provision that specifies a benefit for the surviving spouse of a vested plan participant if the participant dies before retirement. In the United States, qualified plans are required to include this provision, as are registered plans in Canada.

prescribed annuity contract (PAC) In Canada, a kind of annuity that meets the criteria established by the Income Tax Regulations to qualify as exempt from accrual taxation.

prescription drug coverage A type of specified expense coverage that provides benefits for the purchase of drugs and medicines prescribed by a physician and not available over-the-counter.

present value The amount of money that must be invested on a certain day, sometimes called the valuation date, in order to accumulate to a specified amount at a later date.

present value factor   The number by which an amount of money to be paid later is multiplied in order to derive the present value of that money.

present value of amounts not yet due on claims   An amount an insurer sets aside as a reserve for future payments on claims currently being paid in installments, as in the case of disability income coverages and waiver-of-premium benefits.

presumptive disability   A condition that, if present, automatically causes an insured to be considered totally disabled and entitles the insured to receive a disability policy's full income benefit. Examples of presumptive disabilities are total and permanent blindness or loss of two limbs.

pretreatment review provision   See *predetermination of benefits provision.*

prima facie rate   In group creditor insurance in the United States, the standard premium rate recommended by state government regulators for a contributory policy. An insurer can not charge more than the prima facie rate when a contributory group creditor insurance policy is first issued. Contrast with *deviated rate.*

primary beneficiary   The party or parties who have first rights to receive the benefits of a life insurance policy following the death of the insured. Also called *first beneficiary.* Compare to *contingent beneficiary.*

primary care physician (PCP)   A general or family practitioner who serves as the insured's personal physician and first contact with a managed care system.

primary provider of benefits   In a coordination of benefits situation, the medical expense plan that pays the full benefits provided by its plan before any benefits are paid by another medical expense plan.

principal   (1) A sum of money that is invested. (2) A party who authorizes another party, the agent, to act on the principal's behalf in contractual dealings with third parties. Called the *mandator* in Quebec.

probability The likelihood that an event will occur. Probability theory is an essential aspect of the mathematical foundations of insurance.

probationary period See *waiting period.*

proceeds The amount of money that the insurance company is obligated to pay for the settlement of a life insurance policy, endowment insurance policy, or annuity.

professional reinsurer An insurance company whose only or major line of business is reinsurance.

profit sharing pension plan In Canada, a money purchase pension plan in which employer contributions are linked to company profits. Employers must make a minimum contribution of 1 percent of employee earnings, regardless of whether they make a profit, and the plan is subject to the same legal requirements as pension plans.

profit-sharing plan A type of employer-sponsored savings plan that is funded primarily by contributions payable from the employer's profits.

projection method A method of modifying tabular mortality rates in which the insurer multiplies the rate found in a mortality table by a certain fraction or percentage.

property insurance A type of insurance that provides a benefit if insured items are damaged or lost because of fire, theft, accident, or other cause described in the policy.

proportional reinsurance A type of reinsurance plan in which the proportion of the risk to be carried by the ceding company and the proportion of the risk to be carried by the reinsurer are known when the reinsurance treaty is made. Also called *pro rata reinsurance.*

proposal form In Canada, a document that is given to a prospective purchaser of an insurance policy and that contains personalized information about the policy and policy values.

pro rata reinsurance See *proportional reinsurance.*

prospecting The activity of identifying, contacting, and qualifying potential insurance customers.

prospective method A method of calculating policy reserves that looks ahead at a policy's future premiums and benefits and calculates policy reserves using the following equation: *Policy Reserve = Present Value of Future Benefits – Present Value of Future Net Premiums.* See also *retrospective method.*

prospects Potential customers for insurance products.

protective information Information about a proposed insured's impairments that will help the underwriter place the individual in the appropriate risk class.

prototype plan A standardized form of pension or other employee-benefit plan developed to simplify plan drafting for plan sponsors. Similar to a *master plan.*

provider fraud A type of medical insurance fraud that is initiated by a medical care provider on patients' claims in order to increase the provider's own income. Contrast with *individual fraud.*

provision for adverse deviation A liability account that serves as a safety margin to allow for unfavorable variations from actuarial assumptions.

proximate cause of death An event that is directly responsible for a death or an event that initiates an unbroken chain of events that lead to death.

prudent expert rule The legal requirement that the sponsor or manager of a pension plan exhibit certain standards of competence and prudence in accounting for assets in a pension plan and investing the pension plan's funds.

Public Law 15 See *McCarran-Ferguson Act.*

pure broker See *licensed broker.*

pure community rating See *standard community rating.*

pure endowment An amount payable only to those people who survive for a certain period of time; those who do not survive that period of time receive nothing. Unless they are combined with some form of life insurance, pure endowments are generally illegal.

QDRO See *qualified domestic relations order (QDRO).*

QJ&S annuity See *qualified joint and survivor (QJ&S) annuity.*

QPP See *Quebec Pension Plan (QPP).*

qualified annuity In the United States, a type of annuity which is funded with money that is deductible, up to a stated maximum, from the depositor's gross income in the year in which the funds are deposited.

qualified domestic relations order (QDRO) In the United States, a decree or settlement in regard to alimony, child support, or marital property rights that assigns all or a portion of a plan participant's pension benefits to an alternate payee. The alternate payee is generally a spouse, former spouse, or a child or other dependent of the plan participant.

qualified joint and survivor (QJ&S) annuity In the United States, a form of annuity which provides for the continuation of pension benefits to the spouse of a retired pension plan participant after the death of the participant. The survivor's benefits, which cannot be less than 50 percent nor more than 100 percent of the original benefits, continue until the death of the spouse. This form of annuity is required in United States qualified plans, unless the participant (with consent of the spouse) elects to forego it. A similar requirement, called the *joint life and last survivor (JL&S)* option, applies in most Canadian jurisdictions.

qualified plan In the United States, a pension plan or employee-benefit plan that meets a series of federal government requirements and is therefore eligible for certain tax advantages.

qualified preretirement survivor annuity See *preretirement survivor annuity.*

qualifying The process of determining whether a prospect is really a potential customer.

quality business See *well-written business.*

Quebec Pension Plan (QPP) A provincial program that provides a pension for wage earners in Quebec who have contributed money into the plan during their working years. The plan also provides some other benefits including long-term disability benefits. See also *Canada Pension Plan (CPP).*

quota share reinsurance plan A type of reinsurance plan in which the assuming company reinsures a specified percentage of every risk of a certain type insured by the ceding company.

RAA See *retained asset account (RAA).*

rated policy A policy issued to insure a person classified as having a greater-than-average likelihood of loss. The policy may be issued (a) with special exclusions, (b) with a premium rate that is higher than the rate for a standard policy, or (c) with exclusions and a higher than standard premium rate.

rate making The calculation of premium rates for an insurance company's products. Actuaries consider several factors when they establish life insurance premium rates. The most important factors are mortality rates, interest rates, and loading.

rate of return method A method of comparing the costs of life insurance policies wherein the key figure calculated is an annual interest rate, representing a rate of return. Also called the *Linton yield method.* See also *cost comparison methods.*

rating agencies Organizations—independent of any insurer or government body—that evaluate the financial condition of insurers and provide information to potential customers of and investors in insurance companies.

rating classes The three different approaches that insurers take when they use mortality assumptions to calculate group life insurance premiums. The three rating classes for group premiums are manually rated premiums, experience rated premiums, and blended premiums. See also *blended rates, experience rating,* and *manual rates.*

rating manual An abbreviated underwriting manual that includes only suggested ratings and a small amount of background information for each impairment listed.

RBC requirements See *Risk-Based Capital (RBC) requirements.*

RDA See *regional director of agencies (RDA).*

reasonable and customary charge The amount of money most frequently charged for certain medical procedures in a given geographical area. Medical expense insurance payments are often based on reasonable and customary charges.

recapture In reinsurance, the process by which the ceding company takes back from the reinsurer a portion of the reinsured business.

reciprocity In reinsurance, the practice whereby two insurers cede insurance to each other and accept ceded insurance from each other. The insurers often endeavor to cede a near-equal amount of insurance to each other.

recording method A method of changing the beneficiary of a life insurance policy in which the policyowner makes the change effective simply by notifying the insurance company in writing of the change. Also called the *filing method.* Contrast with *endorsement method.*

recovery benefit A partial or residual disability benefit payable after an insured satisfies a qualification or an elimination period, returns to work, and then suffers a loss of earnings directly resulting from a preceding total or partial disability. Also known as *income replacement benefit*. See also *partial disability benefit* and *residual disability benefit*.

redating The process by which an insurer reinstates a term insurance policy without requiring the payment of past due premiums.

reduced paid-up insurance nonforfeiture option A nonforfeiture option under which the net cash value of a life insurance policy is used as a net single premium to purchase a smaller amount of fully paid insurance of the same kind and for the same period as the policy being surrendered.

referred leads Prospect names that an agent receives from a client.

refund annuity An annuity that provides annuity benefits throughout the annuitant's lifetime and guarantees total benefit payments of at least the purchase price of the annuity. See also *cash refund annuity* and *installment refund annuity*.

refund life income option See *life income option with refund*.

regional director of agencies (RDA) An insurance company employee responsible for appointing PPGAs to represent the company.

regional office An insurance company office that provides many of the same functions and operations as the company's home office but is geographically nearer to the market it serves and generally reports to the home office.

registered pension plan (RPP) In Canada, an employer-sponsored pension plan that has been approved by and registered with Revenue Canada.

registered plan In Canada, a private retirement plan that meets the legal requirements to receive favorable tax treatment.

registered principal Any person who is licensed with the National Association of Securities Dealers and who holds a management or supervisory position in a securities broker-dealer firm.

registered reinsurer In Canada, a reinsurer that is licensed to accept reinsurance in a given jurisdiction. Contrast to *unregistered reinsurer.*

registered representative Any person who is licensed with the National Association of Securities Dealers and who is engaged either in selling securities as the agent or representative of a broker-dealer or in training the sales persons associated with a broker-dealer.

registered retirement plan In Quebec, a pension plan that has met the requirements of and has been registered by the Quebec Department of Revenue.

registered retirement savings plan (RRSP) In Canada, an individual retirement account that can be established by any gainfully employed individual. The owner can deduct contributions to an RRSP, up to a stated annual maximum, from his taxable income.

reimbursement benefits See *indemnity benefits.*

reinstatement The process by which an insurer puts back into force a life or health insurance policy that has been terminated for nonpayment of premiums or a life insurance policy that has been continued as extended term or reduced paid-up insurance.

reinstatement provision A life insurance policy provision that describes the conditions the policyowner must meet in order for the insurer to reinstate the policy if it has terminated because of nonpayment of renewal premiums.

reinsurance A type of insurance that one insurance company, known as the *ceding company,* purchases from another insurance company, the *reinsurer,* in order to transfer risks on insurance policies that the ceding company issued.

Reinsurance Guidelines - Canada   See *Canadian Reinsurance Guidelines.*

reinsurance commission An allowance that a reinsurer grants to the ceding company and which is intended to cover part or all of the ceding company's acquisition costs and other costs related to reinsured business.

reinsurance intermediary A third party who negotiates a reinsurance agreement between a reinsurer and a ceding company and may also participate in handling administration and underwriting under the agreement.

reinsurance premium In reinsurance, the consideration paid by a ceding company to an assuming company.

reinsurance treaty A broadly worded statement of an on-going agreement between a reinsurer and a ceding company. The three common types of reinsurance treaties are automatic, facultative, and facultative-obligatory. Usually just called a *treaty.* See also *automatic reinsurance treaty, facultative reinsurance treaty,* and *facultative-obligatory (fac-ob) reinsurance treaty.*

reinsurer An insurance company that accepts the risk transferred from another insurance company in a reinsurance transaction. Also called the *assuming company.*

relation of earnings to insurance clause A clause included in some guaranteed renewable or noncancellable individual disability policies that limits the amount of benefits in which an insurer will participate when the total amount of disability benefits from all insurers exceeds an insured's usual earnings. Also known as a *participation limit.*

relative value schedule A surgical schedule that expresses the cost of a surgical procedure as a unit value rather than as a dollar amount. A procedure with a value of 20, for example, should cost twice as much as a procedure with a value of 10. See also *fee schedule.*

release A document that the recipient of life insurance policy proceeds signs in exchange for those proceeds.

released reserve A policy reserve that is no longer required because the policy is no longer in force.

renewable term insurance A type of term insurance which includes a renewal provision that gives the policyowner the right to renew the insurance coverage at the end of the specified term without submitting evidence of insurability.

renewal commissions Those commissions paid to the agent for a specified number of years, usually nine, after the first policy year. The renewal commission rate is generally much lower than the first-year commission rate and is paid only on policies that remain in force.

renewal premiums Premiums payable after the initial premium.

renewal provision (1) A term life insurance policy provision that gives the policyowner the right to continue the insurance coverage at the end of the specified term without submitting evidence of continued insurability. (2) A provision in an individual health insurance policy describing the circumstances under which the insurance company may refuse to renew the coverage, may cancel the coverage, or may increase the policy's premium rate.

replacement The act of surrendering an insurance policy or part of the coverage of an insurance policy in order to buy another policy.

replacement ratio See *income replacement ratio*.

reportable event In the United States, an event that indicates that the financial condition of a pension plan is or may be deteriorating to the point that the plan may be terminated. Such events must be reported to the Pension Benefit Guaranty Corporation (PBGC).

representation A statement made by a party to an insurance (or other) contract that will invalidate the contract if the statement is not *substantially* true. The statement need not be *literally* true.

required reserve In Canada, a reserve that an insurance company must maintain as required by the insurance department of the province in which the insurer operates and by any foreign jurisdictions in which the insurer operates.

rescission An equitable remedy under which the insurer seeks to void a policy or have it declared void. Rescissions usually occur when there has been material misrepresentation in the insurance application.

reserve Accounts that an insurer maintains to set aside funds for meeting future business obligations. For the reserves identified in this glossary see *active lives reserve, asset valuation reserve (AVR), claim fluctuation reserve, claim reserve, contingency reserve, disabled life reserve, initial reserve, interest maintenance reserve (IMR), mean reserve, midterminal reserve, net level premium reserve, policy reserve, required reserve, reserve for future contingent benefits, statutory policy reserve, terminal reserve,* and *unearned premium reserve.*

reserve destrengthening The process of revaluing and decreasing policy reserves, resulting in an increase in surplus.

reserves for future contingent benefits Additional reserves used for deferred maternity benefits or medical expense policies with high deductibles for which the deductible has nearly been satisfied.

reserve strengthening The process of revaluing and increasing policy reserves, resulting in a decrease in surplus.

reserve valuation (1) The process of establishing a value for an insurer's reserves. (2) The value that is established by actuarial methods for an insurer's reserves.

residual disability benefit A partial disability benefit amount that is established according to a formula specified in a disability income insurance policy. The amount of the benefit varies according to the percentage of income loss attributable to the disability. See also *partial disability benefit.*

resisted claim A claim that an insurer has refused to pay but that it may pay in the future. Also known as a *contested claim* or *disputed claim.*

response letter A direct mail prospecting tool designed to help an agent secure an interview with a prospect. Response letters are semi-personalized letters containing a sales message of general appeal to a large number of people. Prospects indicate their interest by replying to the letter, usually by calling the agent or by returning a coupon or some other inquiry form.

restricted stock Stock that is conditionally given by an employer to compensate an executive. In some instances, the executive is only granted full ownership of the stock if the executive continues to work for the company for a certain period of time.

result clause A type of war hazard exclusion that excludes payment of benefits only for losses resulting from war or acts of war. Contrast with *status clause.*

result-type war exclusion provision See *result clause.*

retail outlet distribution system See *location-selling distribution system.*

retained asset account (RAA) An interest-bearing money market checking account that is established by an insurer for the beneficiary of a life insurance policy, and into which the insurer deposits the policy's death benefit.

retention (1) In reinsurance, the amount of a reinsured risk that the ceding company retains. (2) See *retention charge.*

retention charge For a group insurance contract, the portion of the premium that is intended to cover expenses (other than claims) and contingencies and to allow the insurance company to make a profit. Sometimes simply called *retention.*

retention limit The maximum amount of insurance that an insurance company will carry on any individual without ceding part of the risk to a reinsurer.

retention schedule Part of a reinsurance agreement which specifies the ceding company's retentions for various types of risk. For example, in life reinsurance, retentions will be listed for insureds who fit various age and underwriting classifications.

retired lives reserve A fund that some employers establish and pay into on behalf of employees while they are employed in order to provide group life insurance to the employees after they retire.

retroactive disability benefit A type of disability benefit that is payable from the date of disability. The first payment is not made, however, until an elimination period has been satisfied.

retroactive rate reduction See *experience refund.*

retrocession (1) A transaction in which a reinsurer cedes a portion of its risks to another reinsurer. (2) A parcel or unit of insurance that one reinsurer has assumed and that it cedes to another reinsurer.

retrocessionaire The reinsurance company that accepts the excess risk of another reinsurer.

retro premium In group insurance, a premium rate agreed upon by the insurer and policyholder at the beginning of a premium-paying period but paid at the end of the period only if the group's claim experience warrants it. The insurer collects a lower base premium at the beginning of the period and, if necessary, charges the retro premium retroactively at the end of the period.

retrospective method A method of calculating policy reserves that looks back at a policy's past premiums and benefits to determine policy reserves and that defines the policy reserve for a block of policies according to the following equation: *Policy Reserve = Accumulated Value of Net Premiums − Accumulated Cost of Insurance.* See also *accumulated cost of insurance* and *prospective method.*

retrospective-rating arrangement An alternative funding method for a group insurance contract whereby the insurer collects only a percentage (often between 90 percent and 95 percent) of the premium from the policyholder at the beginning of the premium-paying period and collects the rest of the premium at the end of the period, unless the group's claim experience is better than expected and the additional premium therefore is not owed. With this system the policyholder retains control of part of the premium for a longer time than with the traditional system.

retrospective review   A component of a utilization review program that provides an insurer with periodic reports on physicians' practice patterns and hospitals' average lengths-of-stay.

revocable beneficiary   A named beneficiary whose right to life insurance policy proceeds is not vested during the insured's lifetime and whose designation as beneficiary can be cancelled by the policyowner at any time prior to the insured's death. Contrast with *irrevocable beneficiary.* See also *beneficiary.*

rider   An amendment to an insurance policy that becomes a part of the insurance contract and expands or limits the benefits payable. Also called an *endorsement.*

right of revocation   The policyowner's right to change the beneficiary designation of a life insurance policy.

right of survivorship   In some assignments of life insurance policies, a stipulation which provides that if an assignee dies, the assignee's survivors are entitled to his or her portion of the assignment.

Risk-Based Capital (RBC) requirements   A system used in the United States for evaluating the adequacy of an insurer's capital and surplus based on the insurer's size and the riskiness of its assets and operations.

risk charge   (1) In group insurance, the part of a policy's premium which is intended to contribute to the reserves the insurer maintains to pay for unusually high claims experience. The risk charge is one element of the retention charge. (2) In reinsurance, the amount charged the ceding company by the reinsurer for providing reinsurance.

risk management A system for eliminating or reducing one's exposure to financial risk.

risk class A group of insureds who present a substantially similar risk to the insurance company. Among the most common risk classes used by life insurance companies are standard, preferred, nonsmoker, substandard, and uninsurable.

risk premium reinsurance (RPR) See *yearly renewable term (YRT) reinsurance.*

rollover In the United States, the tax-free transfer of account balances to an individual retirement account from a qualified retirement plan or another individual retirement account.

RPP See *registered pension plan (RPP).*

RPR (risk premium insurance) See *yearly renewable term (YRT) reinsurance.*

RRSP See *registered retirement savings plan (RRSP).*

run-off A termination provision of a reinsurance agreement by virtue of which the reinsurer is liable for losses covered by reinsured policies in force on the date of termination, even if the losses occur after the date of termination. Contrast to *cut-off.*

run on assets A sustained outflow of funds when many customers withdraw their funds from a financial institution within a short period of time. Also called *run on the bank.*

safety margin In life insurance, the safety margin is the amount by which actuaries increase the probability of mortality for each age group in a mortality table. The safety margin helps protect the insurance company from adverse experience.

salaried sales agents Insurance sales representatives who are employees of the insurer and who are usually paid on a salary plus incentive compensation basis. Salaried sales personnel may work with other agents or independently, may make sales directly to consumers or promote the sale of an insurer's products through other intermediaries, and are often used to distribute group insurance and pension products. Also known as *salaried sales representatives.*

salaried sales distribution system   A distribution system that uses salaried employees of the insurance company to sell and service policies. Salaried sales personnel may work either with agents or independently and are often used to distribute group insurance products.

salaried sales representatives   See *salaried sales agents.*

salary continuation plan   A disability or sick-leave plan which provides for employees to continue to receive up to 100 percent of their salary for a limited number of days if they become ill or disabled. The number of days per year granted to an employee generally increases as the employee's length of service increases. Most such plans are self-insured. Also known as a *sick-leave plan.*

salary-reduction plan   A plan whereby an employee authorizes the employer to reduce the amount of compensation that the employee receives in cash and to contribute the difference to a group insurance, pension or other employee-benefit plan.

sales illustration   A graphic representation used by an agent to help explain an insurance product to a potential customer. Sales illustrations often consist of numeric charts describing the customer's goals and the cost elements and mechanics of the insurance product being proposed. Sometimes simply called an *illustration.*

sales tracks   Standardized sales presentations typically used by new or inexperienced agents. Also known as *canned presentations.*

SAP   See *statutory accounting practices (SAP).*

savings bank life insurance (SBLI)   In the United States, life insurance coverage sold by authorized savings banks to people who live or work in the state in which the insurance is sold. Savings bank life insurance is permitted in three states—Massachusetts, New York, and Connecticut.

savings plan See *thrift and savings plan.*

SBLI See *savings bank life insurance (SBLI).*

schedule See *fee schedule.*

scheduled dental plan A dental plan which pays fixed benefits for specific procedures according to a schedule. See also *combination dental plan* and *unscheduled dental plan.*

schedule of benefits See *benefit schedule.*

SCI See *interest-adjusted cost.*

SCI method See *interest adjusted net cost (IANC) method.*

second excess See *second surplus.*

second insured rider A rider that may be added to a permanent life insurance policy to provide term insurance coverage on the life of an individual other than the policy's insured. Also known as an *optional insured rider* or *additional insured rider.*

second surgical opinion (SSO) program A cost-containment technique used by some medical expense insurance plans under which insureds who are considering elective surgery must get another physician's professional opinion as to the medical necessity of the surgical procedure.

second surplus In a layered reinsurance agreement, the amount of risk ceded in the second layer. See also *layering.* Also called *second excess.*

second-to-die life insurance See *last survivor life insurance.*

secondary beneficiary See *contingent beneficiary.*

Section 79 Section 79 of the United States Internal Revenue Code, which provides that employer contributions to purchase group term life insurance receive preferable tax treatment. It also gives a list of specifications which a plan must meet in order to be considered a nondiscriminatory group term insurance plan for tax purposes.

Section 401(k) Plan In the United States, a qualified cash or deferred profit-sharing or stock-bonus plan which allows participants to decide, within limits, how much of their compensation is deferred. Participant contributions are not taxable until the funds are withdrawn, and sponsor contributions as well as investment earnings are also tax-deferred to the participant. Also called a *Cash or Deferred Arrangement (CODA)*.

Section 403(b) Plan In the United States, a type of employee retirement plan established by certain tax-exempt organizations (i.e., hospitals, charities, churches) and educational organizations. Section 403(b) plans were created by Congress to serve as an incentive for tax-exempt organizations (who could not benefit from the tax advantages of qualified pension plans) to offer their employees some form of retirement compensation. Also known as a *tax-deferred annuity (TDA) plan* or a *tax-sheltered annuity (TSA) plan*.

Section 415 limits In the United States, limits placed on the amount of annual additions (contributions) that can be made on behalf of a defined contribution plan participant or the amount of benefits that can be paid to a participant in a defined benefit plan. These limits are determined under Section 415 of the Internal Revenue Code. See also *contribution limit* and *maximum benefit*.

Section 3460 In Canada, a set of recommendations contained in section 3460 of the Canadian Institute of Chartered Accounts (CICA) Handbook. The recommendations concern employers' accounting for pension costs and obligations. Section 3460 recommends that, for defined benefit plans, the projected benefit method be used to determine pension costs for accounting purposes.

segmentation A process by which an insurer divides its general account investments into distinct parts, or segments, that correspond with each of the insurer's major lines of business. For example, one segment can be used to account for group life insurance investments, while another can be used to account for individual life insurance investments.

segregated account In Canada, an investment account maintained separately from an insurer's general investment account to help manage the funds placed in variable life insurance policies and variable annuities. Called a *separate account* in the United States. See also *general account* and *investment-sensitive life insurance*.

select and ultimate mortality table A mortality table that shows select mortality experience as well as the ultimate mortality experience that follows the select period. See also *mortality table* and *select mortality table*.

select group Applicants who have recently been accepted for life insurance at standard rates. For a given period after being accepted, the mortality rate of the select group is better than the mortality rate of the general population.

selection against the insurer See *antiselection*.

selection of risks See *underwriting*.

select mortality table A mortality table that shows only the mortality experience of people who have recently been accepted for life insurance (a *select group*.) The mortality rates shown in a select mortality table are based on both the age of the insured at the time the policy was issued and the period of time since the insurance was issued. See also *mortality table* and *select and ultimate mortality table*.

select period The period of years during which there is a significant difference in mortality rates between persons whose good health was proved at the beginning of the period (the select group) and other persons of the same age.

self-administered group insurance plan   Under this type of group insurance plan, the group policyholder rather than the insurer performs most of the administrative work for the plan. The policyholder maintains detailed records of group membership, processes routine requests, such as requests for beneficiary changes and name and address changes, prepares its own premium statements, and, in some cases, prepares certificates for new group members. See also *insurer-administered group insurance plan.*

self-administration   In reinsurance, a system of administration whereby the ceding company prepares the majority of the records for cessions, and uses written or electronic lists, often called bordereaux, to notify the reinsurer of cessions. See also *bordereau.* Contrast to *individual cession administration.*

self-insurance   A risk-management technique by which a person or business accepts financial responsibility for losses associated with specific risks.

self-insured group insurance plan   A form of group insurance in which the group sponsor, not an insurance company, is financially responsible for paying claims made by group insureds. A group may be partially or fully self insured. See also *administrative services only (ASO) contract.* Contrast with *fully-insured group insurance plan.*

sentinel effect   The tendency of hospitals involved in hospital audit programs to carefully prepare hospital bills because they expect their bills to be reviewed in detail by insurers.

SEP   See *simplified employee pension (SEP).*

separate account   In the United States, an investment account maintained separately from an insurer's general investment account to help manage the funds placed in variable life insurance policies and variable annuities. Called a *segregated account* in Canada. See also *general account* and *investment-sensitive life insurance.*

separate account contract A retirement plan funding vehicle in which the plan's assets are invested in an insurer's separate account. A separate account contract usually does not guarantee investment performance. Also called an *investment facility contract.*

SERP See *supplemental executive retirement plan (SERP).*

service and claim department See *customer service department.*

service benefits Medical expense insurance plan benefits that are stated in terms of the services that will be provided by the plan. Contrast with *indemnity benefits.* Blue Cross and Blue Shield plans traditionally provide service benefits. Many commercial insurers now provide service benefits.

service fee A form of agent compensation that constitutes a small percentage of the premium and that is usually payable only after renewal commissions on a policy have ceased. Also called a *persistency fee.*

setback The number of years sometimes subtracted from the true age in life insurance mortality tables. A setback is sometimes used with male mortality tables when an insurer needs to calculate mortality rates for females.

settlement (1) See *financial settlement.* (2) In the United States, an irrevocable action that relieves the plan or plan sponsor of the obligation for a pension benefit and that eliminates the risk to the plan assets used to carry out the settlement. One example of a settlement is payment of a lump-sum benefit to a plan participant, thus discharging any further benefit obligation to the participant. Settlement is defined in FASB Statement No. 88.

settlement agreement The arrangement made between an insurer and a life insurance policyowner concerning the manner in which the insurer will pay the policy proceeds to the beneficiary. See also *settlement options.*

settlement option payments Periodic payments made by an insurance company in lieu of an immediate lump-sum payment of life insurance policy proceeds.

settlement options Choices available to the policyowner or the beneficiary of a life insurance policy regarding the method by which the insurer will pay policy proceeds. Also known as *optional modes of settlement.* See also *fixed amount option, fixed period option, interest option, joint and survivorship option, life income option, life income option with period certain, life income option with refund,* and *straight life income option.*

settlement options provision A life insurance policy provision that grants a policyowner or beneficiary several choices as to how the policy proceeds will be distributed.

settlement option table A table showing the various amounts that the insurance company will pay as periodic payments in the settlement of a life insurance policy.

sex-distinct mortality table A mortality table that shows different mortality rates for males and females, reflecting the fact that women, as a group, experience lower mortality at all ages than men.

shopping In facultative reinsurance, the practice of submitting an application to several reinsurers in order to obtain the best underwriting rating or the lowest overall cost for the policy in question.

short-form reinstatement application A reinstatement application that asks a few questions designed to guard against the reinstatement of a policy when the insured's condition has changed drastically since the premium due date. A short-form reinstatement application is generally used for reinstatements requested within a comparatively short period, such as 30 to 90 days after the end of the grace period.

short-term disability income insurance Disability income insurance that provides a benefit for a short disability or for the first part of a long disability. Group short-term disability generally specifies a maximum benefit period of less than one year, commonly 13, 26, or 52 weeks. Individual short-term disability insurance features a maximum benefit period of from one to five years. See also *disability income insurance, long-term disability income insurance,* and *weekly indemnity plan.*

sick-leave plan See *salary continuation plan.*

side fund See *conversion fund.*

simplified employee pension (SEP) In the United States, a pension plan in which an employer contributes money to an individual retirement account (IRA) for each employee covered by the plan. The IRA is owned by the employee, not the employer. A SEP is especially useful to employers who cannot afford the time or money needed to administer and maintain a more complicated pension plan. SEPs may also be used by self-employed persons.

simultaneous death act A state or provincial law which provides that if the insured and the primary beneficiary both die under conditions in which it is impossible to determine which one died first, the insured will be presumed to have survived the primary beneficiary unless there is a policy provision to the contrary.

single-need selling A basis for selling life insurance in which the agent isolates one of a prospect's financial needs that can be met by insurance. For example, the agent may point out to a prospect the need for sufficient life insurance to cover the outstanding balance on the prospect's home mortgage. Contrast to *total-needs programming.*

single premium annuity An annuity that is purchased with only one premium payment. A single premium annuity can be an immediate annuity or a deferred annuity.

single-premium deferred annuity (SPDA) A deferred annuity for which only one premium payment is made.

single-premium immediate annuity (SPIA) See *immediate annuity.*

single-premium method In group creditor insurance, a premium-paying arrangement for contributory plans whereby, at the inception of the loan, the entire premium amount for the insurance is either paid in a lump sum by the borrower or added to the principal of the loan. Contrast with *monthly outstanding balance method.*

single-premium whole life insurance Whole life insurance purchased with a single, lump-sum premium.

single purchase annuity contract A group contract in which a single premium is applied to purchase annuities for participants in a pension plan that is terminating. Immediate annuities are purchased for current retirees in the plan, and deferred annuities are purchased for participants who have not yet reached retirement age.

six and six exclusion In credit disability policies, a pre-existing conditions exclusion which states that an insured's disability is not covered if the insured (1) was treated for the condition within six months prior to the effective date of coverage and (2) becomes disabled from that same condition within six months after the effective date of coverage.

small estates statutes Legislation that enables an insurer to pay relatively small amounts of policy proceeds to an estate without involved court proceedings.

small group insurance plan A type of group life insurance plan that uses group underwriting techniques but adds some degree of simplified individual underwriting and is designed to cover groups containing 2 to 25 people. Also called a *baby group plan.*

small life insurance company deduction A United States federal income tax deduction that may be used by certain life insurance companies if they meet criteria relating to the amount of the company's assets and tentative life insurance company taxable income, or LICTI.

social insurance supplement coverage Medical expense insurance sold by insurance companies to provide benefits that supplement the benefits available from a specified government health insurance program.

Social Security   In the United States, a federal program that provides monthly income benefits to qualified workers who retire or become disabled and to the surviving spouses and dependent children of covered workers who have died.

Social Security Disability Income (SSDI)   In the United States, a long-term disability income program that provides benefits to disabled workers who are under age 65 and who have paid a specified amount of Social Security tax for a prescribed number of quarter-year periods.

sole proprietorship insurance   Insurance on the life of the sole proprietor of a business. Sole proprietorship insurance is used either to pay the salary of someone hired to run the business after the owner's death or disablement or to compensate the owner's family for the loss of potential income due to the failure of the business after the owner's death or disability.

soliciting agent   Typically, an insurance agent who works under a general agent or a branch manager. The soliciting agent is the person who actually contacts prospective customers, delivers policies, and collects initial premiums. See also *insurance agent.*

solvency   An insurer's ability to pay its debts and to pay policy benefits when they come due. Also called *economic solvency* or *technical solvency.*

SPD   See *Summary Plan Description (SPD).*

SPDA   See *single-premium deferred annuity (SPDA).*

SPIA (single-premium immediate annuity)   See *immediate annuity.*

special class risks   See *substandard risk class.*

special surplus fund   Surplus that a life insurance company's board of directors has set aside for the purpose of meeting unforeseen contingencies or paying for certain extraordinary expenses that may arise. Also called *appropriated surplus, assigned surplus, contingency reserve,* and *earmarked surplus.*

specific stop-loss coverage See *individual stop-loss coverage.*

specified expense coverage Medical expense insurance coverage that provides benefits for specific medical supplies or treatments or for specific illnesses. Examples include dental expense coverage, vision care coverage, prescription drug coverage, long-term care (LTC) coverage and dread disease coverage.

speculative underwriting The practice of knowingly accepting risks at an inadequate premium rate in order to obtain business by undercutting the market price for similar coverage.

speedy issue unit See *jet unit.*

spendthrift trust clause A life insurance policy provision that protects, under certain conditions, policy proceeds held by the insurer from being seized by a beneficiary's creditors.

split-dollar insurance plan A type of business insurance in which an employee is covered by individual life insurance that is paid for jointly by the employee and the employer. The employee names the beneficiaries. Each year the employer pays the portion of the premium that is equal to the increase in the policy's cash value for that year, and the employee pays the balance of the premium. If the employee dies, the employer will receive an amount of the proceeds equal to the cash value of the policy, while the beneficiaries of the policy will receive the remaining benefits.

split funding A method of funding a pension plan in which a portion of the total contributions to the plan are used to purchase an allocated funding instrument while the remainder of the contributions are placed in an unallocated fund.

spouse and children's insurance rider A rider that may be added to a permanent life insurance policy to provide term insurance coverage on the insured's spouse and children.

spouse's allowance In Canada, a benefit available to some spouses of Old Age Security (OAS) recipients. The benefit is designed to ensure that a married couple in which one spouse is age 60 to 65 receives a minimum monthly pension that is comparable to the monthly pension of a married couple in which both spouses are over the age of 65.

spread loss reinsurance A type of reinsurance by virtue of which the reinsured company pays premiums to the reinsurer and, if the reinsured company experiences total losses in a given year which are greater than a certain limit, then the reinsurer remits the amount of the excess loss to the reinsured company in a lump sum, and the reinsured company pays back the reinsurer over a period of years, usually by means of increased reinsurance premiums. In this way, the reinsured company's losses for a certain year are "spread" over a period of years. This type of insurance is seen more frequently in group insurance than in individual insurance.

SSDI See *Social Security Disability Income (SSDI).*

SSO program See *second surgical opinion (SSO) program.*

stacking The practice of ignoring benefits payable under public pension plans in the design or selection of private pension plans. When no attempt is made to integrate benefits from a public and a private pension plan, the two plans are said to be "stacked."

staff-model HMO A type of closed-panel HMO that directly employs physicians to provide services to HMO members.

standard community rating A system in which a health plan charges the same premium to all members. Also called *pure community rating.*

Standard Nonforfeiture Law   A law, which is virtually uniform in all states, specifying the minimum cash values required to be provided by life insurance policies.

standard plan termination   In pension and employee-benefit plan terms, the process of terminating a plan that has sufficient funds to cover all the benefit amounts to which the plan's participants are entitled. Contrast to *distress termination.* See also *involuntary plan termination* and *voluntary plan termination.*

standard premium rate   The premium rate charged for insurance on a member of the standard risk class.

standard risk class   A risk class made up of individuals whose anticipated likelihood of loss is not significantly higher or lower than average. Most insureds are included in the standard risk class.

Standard Valuation Law   A law, which is virtually uniform in all states, specifying minimum standards for calculating, or valuing, insurance reserves. See also *Amendments to the Standard Valuation Law.*

status clause   A type of war hazard exclusion that excludes payment of benefits for any loss occurring while an insured is in military service. Contrast with *result clause.*

status-type war exclusion provision   See *status clause.*

statutory accounting practices (SAP)   A set of financial accounting standards that all United States life and health insurers must follow when preparing the Annual Statement and certain other financial reports.

statutory policy reserve   In the United States, policy reserves established to satisfy the requirements of state insurance regulators. Also called *legal reserve.* See also *policy reserve.*

statutory solvency   An insurer's ability to maintain at least the minimum amount of capital and surplus specified by insurance regulators.

stock bonus plan An employee-benefit plan whereby part of the employees' compensation is in the form of the employer's stock. Most stock bonus plans are maintained in the same fashion as profit-sharing plans, but the employer's stock contributions are not necessarily related to profits. As with profit-sharing plans, employer contributions are most often discretionary, and the plan may not be intended as a retirement plan.

stock dividend See *dividend.*

stock insurance company An insurance company that is owned by people who buy shares of the company's stock. Contrast with *mutual insurance company.*

stock option incentive An incentive plan for executives whereby an employer offers to sell the company's stock to the executive at a certain price on a certain date. It is in the executive's interest for the company to do well and the stock's value to rise. If the stock's value does rise, the executive may, by exercising the stock option, be able to buy the company's stock at a price below the stock's market value, thus making a paper profit (if the stock is or must be held) or a realized profit (if the stock is sold at the higher price).

stock repurchase insurance Life insurance intended to finance the purchase of stock from the estate of a deceased stockholder by other stockholders in the same company. Typically used for closely-held corporations that have few stockholders. See also *business-continuation insurance.*

stop-loss insurance A type of insurance coverage under which the sponsor of a self-insured group health insurance plan is reimbursed for covered claims that exceed a stated dollar limit. See *aggregate stop-loss coverage* and *individual stop-loss coverage.*

stop-loss provision A health insurance policy provision specifying that the insurer will pay 100 percent of the insured's eligible medical expenses after the insured has incurred a specified amount of out-of-pocket expenses in deductible and coinsurance payments.

stop-loss reinsurance plan A type of nonproportional reinsurance plan in which the ceding company pays all claims as they occur during a specified period, such as one year, up to a certain amount, called the attachment point. At the end of the period, the reinsurer pays the ceding company an agreed-upon percentage of the claims in excess of the attachment point up to a stated maximum per period. Stop-loss coverage affects only the portion of each risk retained by the ceding company. Amounts in excess of the company's retention limit are reinsured under other arrangements.

straight life annuity An annuity that provides periodic payments to the annuitant for as long as the annuitant lives and that provides for no benefit payments after the annuitant's death.

straight life income option A life insurance policy settlement option under which payments to the beneficiary-payee will continue until the payee's death, after which no further payments are made.

straight life insurance See *continuous-premium whole life insurance.*

substandard broker A general agent who runs a brokerage shop specializing in finding coverage for substandard cases or selling the products of several insurers with expertise in underwriting substandard risks.

substandard premium rate The premium rate charged for insurance on an insured person classified as having a greater than average likelihood of loss. This premium rate is higher than a standard premium rate.

substandard risk class A risk class made up of people with medical or nonmedical impairments that give them a greater than average likelihood of loss. Substandard risks pay higher-than-standard premiums. Members of this risk class are called *special class risks.*

succession beneficiary clause See *preference beneficiary clause.*

successor beneficiary See *contingent beneficiary.*

successor owner A person designated to become the owner of a life insurance policy if the owner dies before the person insured by the policy dies. In Quebec, known as the *contingent owner.*

successor payee See *contingent payee.*

suicide clause Life insurance policy wording which specifies that the proceeds of the policy will not be paid if the insured takes his or her own life within a specified period of time (usually two years) after the policy's date of issue. Also called *suicide exclusion provision.*

summary information folder In Canada, a document that is used in marketing variable life insurance products. The document discloses all of the material facts about the particular variable contract and contains certain statements of financial information about the contract's segregated funds.

Summary Plan Description (SPD) (1) In the United States, a document required by ERISA to provide information about a pension plan to plan participants in simple language. The SPD must, among other requirements, identify the plan's administrator and those who are responsible for managing the plan's assets, must explain the plan's eligibility requirements and the circumstances under which a plan participant could forfeit his or her benefits under the plan, and must explain the procedures for making claims under the plan. (2) In the United States, a description of various aspects of a group insurance plan. An SPD must be provided to all plan participants and to the Department of Labor.

superimposed major medical plan A major medical plan that is coordinated with various basic medical expense coverages and that provides benefits for expenses that exceed these coverages.

superintendent of agencies Under the home service distribution system, the administrative link between the home office and the district offices.

Superintendent's Guidelines In Canada, a series of recommendations made by the Canadian Council of Insurance Regulators (CCIR) to insurance companies concerning a variety of matters, such as variable life insurance contracts, health insurance contracts, and group insurance contracts.

superstandard risk class See *preferred risk class.*

supplemental executive retirement plan (SERP) A nonqualified deferred compensation retirement plan designed to provide benefits for a group of executives, without regard to benefits provided under a qualified retirement plan.

supplemental group life insurance Life insurance over and above the basic coverage provided by a group policy. The supplemental coverage may provide an additional amount of the same type of insurance or may provide a different type of insurance. Supplemental coverage is usually contributory and subject to stricter underwriting standards than is the basic group coverage.

supplemental insurance coverage Optional group insurance coverage that may be offered in addition to a basic group insurance plan.

supplemental major medical insurance Major medical insurance that supplements an underlying basic medical expense insurance policy. Together, supplemental major medical and basic medical insurance should cover most of an insured's medical expenses. See also *basic medical expense coverage.*

supplementary benefit rider A rider that is added to an insurance policy to provide additional benefits. Some typical supplementary benefit riders are accidental death coverage, waiver of premium, and the guaranteed insurance option. See also *rider.*

supplementary contract A contract between the insurer and the beneficiary of a life insurance policy. A supplementary contract is formed when policy proceeds are applied under a settlement option.

supplementary contract with life contingencies (WLC) A supplementary contract or annuity in which the duration of the payment period depends on the lifetime of the beneficiary.

supplementary contract without life contingencies (WOLC) A supplementary contract or annuity in which the proceeds of a life insurance policy are held at interest or paid in installments over a specified period.

supplementary notice As required by the Fair Credit Reporting Act, notice to a consumer of the nature and scope of the investigation mentioned in the pre-notice form that an insurance company has already sent to the consumer.

supplementary statement Under the NAIC Model Privacy Act, a written statement made by a person who has been investigated. The supplementary statement is intended to correct what the investigated person believes to be incorrect information in his or her file. This statement must remain with the disputed information in the person's file and must be made available to anyone reviewing the disputed information.

surgical schedule The part of a health insurance policy that describes the maximum benefit amounts payable for specified surgical procedures. See also *fee schedule* and *relative value schedule.*

surgical expense coverage See *basic medical expense coverage.*

surplus The amount by which an insurance company's assets exceed its liabilities and capital.

surplus brokers See *agent-brokers.*

surplus relief In financial reinsurance, the situation that occurs when an insurance company cedes insurance to a reinsurer and, because it no longer maintains reserve liability accounts for the ceded insurance, increases its surplus for statutory accounting purposes. It is generally accepted that an insurance company's insurance in force (or "premiums written") should not exceed a certain proportion of its surplus. If, at any time, the insurer decides that its surplus is not sufficient for this criterion to be met, the insurer may seek surplus relief.

surplus strain The decrease in an insurer's capital and surplus caused by high first-year costs and the reserving requirements associated with new products. Also called *issue strain* or *new business strain.*

surrender charge (1) Expense charges sometimes imposed when a policyowner surrenders a universal life policy. (2) A charge imposed if the contractowner surrenders a deferred annuity policy within a stated number of years after it was purchased.

surrender cost index (SCI) See *interest-adjusted cost.*

surrender cost index (SCI) method See *interest adjusted net cost (IANC) method.*

survivor benefit A benefit provided by most deferred annuity policies under which the annuity's accumulated value is paid to a designated beneficiary if the annuitant or contractowner dies before annuity benefit payments begin. Also called *death benefit.*

survivor income benefit insurance A type of group life insurance which provides income benefits if the insured is survived by a "qualified survivor." Usually the qualified survivor category includes only the insured's spouse and children.

survivorship clause See *common disaster clause.*

survivorship life insurance See *last survivor life insurance.*

suspense account In insurance accounting, an account used to record transactions that cannot be credited immediately to a permanent account. For example, when a company receives a premium payment in advance for a policy not yet issued, it records the payment in a premium suspense account.

switch See *flip-flop.*

tabular cost of insurance The amount deducted from the policy reserve of each life insurance policy at the end of a year to help pay the death claims made on other policies during that year. The word "tabular" refers to the fact that this cost is calculated using the same mortality table and interest rate that are used in the calculation of net premiums and reserves.

tabular interest rate The interest rate used to calculate a policy's reserves.

tabular mortality See *expected mortality.*

tabular mortality rate The rate of death at any given age, as shown in the mortality table that is used to calculate life insurance premium rates.

Taft-Hartley Trust See *negotiated trusteeship.*

TAP See *Trend Analysis Program (TAP).*

target-benefit pension plan A defined contribution plan where the contribution amount is designed to provide the participant with a specific (or "target") benefit. However, the sponsor does not guarantee the benefit, so no adjustment is made if actual investment results (or other variables) differ from initial projections. At retirement, the funds in the employee's account may be paid in a lump sum or used to purchase an annuity.

tax-deferred annuity (TDA) plan See *Section 403(b) Plan.*

Tax Equity and Fiscal Responsibility Act of 1982 (TEFRA) United States federal legislation designed to increase tax revenues through a variety of means such as restrictions on the tax deductibility of certain investments, including some life insurance and pension products, and the elimination of distinctions in tax law applicable to partnerships and sole proprietorships.

tax-sheltered annuity (TSA) plan See *Section 403(b) Plan.*

TDA See *Section 403(b) Plan.*

team underwriting An underwriting approach in which the underwriting department is divided into small, independent groups composed of underwriters and processing clerks.

technical solvency See *solvency.*

TEFRA See *Tax Equity and Fiscal Responsibility Act of 1982 (TEFRA).*

TEFRA corridor See *corridor.*

temporary insurance agreements Legal agreements between an insurer and a proposed insured that provide a guaranteed amount of temporary life insurance coverage for a specific period of time, usually the underwriting period. Also known as *interim insurance agreements* and *temporary insurance receipts.*

temporary life annuity An annuity that provides periodic benefit payments until the end of a specified number of years or until the annuitant's death, whichever comes first.

ten-day free look See *free examination period.*

terminal illness (TI) benefit An accelerated death benefit provided by some individual life insurance policies under which the insurer pays a portion of the policy's death benefit to a policyowner-insured who suffers from a terminal illness and has a life expectancy of 12 months or less.

terminal policy dividend An extra dividend or pro-rata dividend covering the period between the last policy anniversary date and the termination date of the policy.

terminal reserve The reserve on a policy at the end of a policy year.

termination expenses The cost of processing death benefit claims and cash surrenders.

term insurance Life insurance under which the benefit is payable only if the insured dies during a specified period. See also *convertible term insurance, credit life insurance, decreasing term insurance, deposit term insurance, family income insurance, increasing term insurance, level term insurance, mortgage redemption insurance,* and *renewable term insurance.*

territory (1) The geographical area for which a home service agent has exclusive responsibility. Home service districts are divided into territories. Also called an *account,* an *agency,* or a *debit.* (2) The geographical area for which an insurance agent or general agent has responsibility.

testamentary disposition In life insurance, the use of a will to indicate the person or party to whom the proceeds of a life insurance policy should be distributed.

third-party administrator (TPA) An organization that administers group benefit plans for self-insured groups but that does not have financial responsibility for paying benefits. TPAs may also offer advice to clients on the purchase and design of employee benefits programs. The self-insured group pays its own benefits. See also *administrative services only (ASO) contract* and *self-insured group insurance.*

third-party application An insurance application submitted by a person or party other than the proposed insured.

third-party endorsement A method of marketing individual insurance to groups. In the third-party endorsement method, a life insurance company makes an agreement with an organization (such as a club, a business, or a professional association) to sell individual insurance to members or employees of the organization. The organization endorses the insurer's products, but the group members are free to buy the products or not.

third-party insurance   Insurance that one person purchases on the life of another.

13-month rate   A lapse rate that is computed on the basis of the proportion of new policies on which no part of any required second year premium has been paid. Companies use a 13-month rate, rather than a one-year rate, because most lapses of policies purchased on an annual premium mode occur when the first renewal premium remains unpaid at the end of the policy's 13th month in force.

three-factor contribution method   A method for calculating policy dividends, considering separately the contributions arising from interest, mortality, and loading.

thrift and savings plan   A type of contributory savings plan to which an employer is obligated to make contributions on behalf of an employee if that employee makes a specified contribution to the plan. A 401(k) plan is a special type of thrift and savings plan.

thrift plan   See *thrift and savings plan.*

TI benefit   See *terminal illness (TI) benefit.*

time clause   See *common disaster clause.*

time limit on certain defenses provision   A health insurance policy clause that provides a time limit on the insurer's right to dispute a policy's validity based on material misstatements made in the application.

TNC method   See *traditional net cost (TNC) method.*

top-heavy plan   In the United States, a pension plan or employee-benefit plan which provides more than 60 percent of its accrued benefits to the owners, executives or most highly paid employees of a company (known as key employees). To remain qualified, a top-heavy plan must provide certain minimum benefits to nonkey employee participants. See also *key employee.*

total disability A disability that meets the definition in a disability income policy and that entitles the insured to receive full disability income benefits. When a disability begins, it is typically considered a "total disability" if it prevents an insured person from performing the essential duties of his or her regular occupation. Under many insurance policies, the definition of total disability changes at the end of a specified period after the disability begins, usually two years. Thereafter, insureds are considered totally disabled only if their disabilities prevent them from working at any occupation for which they are reasonably fitted by education, training, or experience. See also *disability.*

total-needs programming A basis for selling life insurance in which the agent takes into consideration all the prospect's financial needs, calculates the amount of money required to take care of all those needs, determines the amount of funds that will be available when the prospect dies, and calculates the amount of life insurance required to provide the difference. Sometimes called *financial planning.* Contrast to *single-need selling.*

TPA See *third-party administrator (TPA).*

traditional cession administration See *individual cession administration.*

traditional net cost (TNC) method An insurance policy cost comparison method that is prohibited by the NAIC Model Life Insurance Solicitation Regulation primarily because it ignores the time value of money.

training allowances Subsidy or salary plans that are used to compensate new, inexperienced agents. Also known as *development allowances.*

travel accident benefit An accidental death benefit often included in group insurance policies issued to employer-employee groups. This benefit is payable only if an accident occurs while an employee is traveling for the employer.

treaty See *reinsurance treaty.*

Trend Analysis Program (TAP) An ACLI research program which studies emerging social and other trends in the United States that may be significant to the life and health insurance business.

trial application See *preliminary inquiry form.*

triple indemnity A type of accidental death benefit coverage that pays an additional benefit equal to twice the policy's basic death benefit if the accident is sustained while the insured is a passenger in a public conveyance operated by a licensed common carrier, such as a bus, train, or airplane.

trust agreement In a trusteed pension plan, the contract between the plan sponsor and the trustee that describes the trustee's authority and responsibilities for investing and administering plan assets. Trust agreements are also found when group insurance is provided through a multiple-employer trust (MET).

trusteed group insurance plan A type of self-insured group health insurance plan under which covered claims and expenses are paid from a trust established by the employer. See also *general asset plan.*

trusteed pension plan A pension plan in which the plan sponsor chooses a trustee to be responsible for investing the plan's assets or for choosing an investor for the plan's assets. Also known as a *pension trust.*

trust fund plan A pension plan under which employer and employee contributions are forwarded to a trustee, who is responsible for investing the contributions and is often responsible for making benefit payments to plan participants. The duties of the trustee, who may be an individual or an institution such as a bank trust department, are spelled out in a trust agreement. A trustee generally does not guarantee that the trust fund will be adequate to pay current and future pension benefits.

TSA See *Section 403(b) Plan.*

twisting A prohibited insurance sales practice that occurs when an agent induces a policyowner to cancel an insurance policy and use the cash value of that policy to buy a new policy, when doing so is not in the policyowner's best interests.

UCR fee See *usual, customary, and reasonable (UCR) fee.*

ultimate cost The total net cost, including the cost of all benefits and expenses, incurred by a pension plan over the life span of the plan.

ultimate mortality table A mortality table that shows mortality rates for people who have not recently been underwritten. See also *mortality table* and *select mortality table.*

unallocated funding A method of funding a pension plan in which the pension funds as a whole are held and managed by a funding agency, often an insurance company, and are not allocated to specific plan participants. When a participant retires, the funding agency either purchases an annuity for the retiree or pays periodic benefits directly from the fund. However, the funding agency makes no contractual promises that it will pay any specific benefit amounts. Contrast with *allocated funding.*

unappropriated earned surplus In Canada, the amount of an insurer's surplus remaining after determination of an insurer's reserves, capital, and other surplus amounts.

unassigned surplus The amount of surplus remaining after the creation of any special surplus funds.

unauthorized reinsurer In the United States, a reinsurer that is not authorized by the regulatory authorities in the direct writing insurer's state of domicile.

unbundled insurance product An insurance product in which the mortality, investment, and expense factors used to calculate premium rates and cash values are each identified in the policy. Some nontraditional products, such as universal life insurance, are unbundled. See also *bundled insurance product.*

unclaimed benefits   Policy benefits for which no payee can be found. Under typical state statutes for unclaimed property, when an insurer cannot locate anyone entitled to policy benefits, the insurer will hold the unclaimed benefits for seven years and then turn them over to the state. Usually, the unclaimed property statute of the state of the beneficiary's last known address applies. If no address is known, the statute of the insurer's state of domicile will govern.

unclaimed property statutes   Statutes that regulate the disposition of funds for which no owner can be found. Insurers typically hold unclaimed property for seven years. If the rightful owner is not found during this time, the property is turned over to the state. Also known as *escheat laws*. See also *unclaimed benefits*.

uncollected premiums   In the United States, life insurance premiums and annuity considerations that are due on or before the Annual Statement date but that have not been received by that date.

underlying   In reinsurance, the amount of insurance assumed on a risk before the next layer of reinsurance comes into effect. See *layering*.

underwriter   (1) The person who assesses and classifies the degree of risk that a proposed insured represents. (2) The person or organization that guarantees that money will be available to pay for losses that are insured against. In this sense, the insurance company is the underwriter.

underwriting   (1) The process of assessing and classifying the degree of risk that a proposed insured represents. Also called *selection of risks*. (2) Providing guarantees that money will be available to pay for losses that are insured against.

underwriting at point of sale   See *immediate underwriting*.

underwriting department   The department in a life and health insurance company that selects the risks that the company will insure. The underwriting department tries to make sure that the actual mortality or morbidity rates of the company's insureds do not exceed the rates assumed when premium rates were calculated. The underwriter considers an applicant's age, weight, physical condition, personal and family medical history, occupation, financial resources, and other selection factors to determine the degree of risk represented by the proposed insured. This department also participates in the negotiation and management of reinsurance agreements, through which an insurance company transfers some or all of an insurance risk to another insurance company. Also called the *new business department.*

underwriting guidelines General rules that an underwriting staff uses in assigning applicants to an insurance company's different premium classifications.

underwriting impairments Factors that tend to increase an individual's risk above that which is normal for his or her age.

underwriting manual A summary of the methods used by a particular insurer to evaluate and rate risks. The underwriting manual provides underwriters with background information on underwriting impairments and serves as a guide to suggested underwriting actions when various impairments are present. See also *risk class.*

underwriting requirements Printed instructions that indicate what evidence of insurability is required for a given situation and which of several optional information sources will be needed to provide underwriters with necessary information. Sources of information may include medical records and the results of physical examinations. Underwriting requirements are graduated based on the proposed insured's age and the amount of coverage requested.

underwriting worksheet A printout of all available information about a proposed insured and, in some companies, pertinent information about the agent who submitted the application.

unearned premium reserve A liability account that includes premiums paid for coverage occurring in a future accounting period.

Unemployment Insurance Act In Canada, a federal statute that provides unemployment insurance to almost all persons who are employed in Canada. Benefits are provided to covered employees who are laid off or unable to work due to accidental injury, sickness, or pregnancy.

Uniform Accident and Sickness Insurance Act In Canada, model legislation governing health insurance contracts agreed upon by the Canadian Council of Insurance Regulators (CCIR) and enacted with minor variations by all the common law jurisdictions.

Uniform Life Insurance Act In Canada, model legislation governing life insurance and annuity contracts agreed upon by the Canadian Council of Insurance Regulators (CCIR) and enacted with minor variations by all of the common law jurisdictions.

Uniform Pension Plan (UPP) In Canada, a prototype pension plan (see *prototype plan*) developed by members of the Canadian Life and Health Insurance Association and approved by the appropriate Canadian regulatory authorities, including Revenue Canada.

unilateral contract A contract in which only one party makes legally enforceable promises when entering into the contract. A life insurance policy is a unilateral contract.

uninsurable risk class The group of people with a risk of loss so great that an insurance company will not offer them insurance.

union welfare fund or **union welfare trust** A fund organized by a union and one or more employers to which contributions are made by the employer(s) so that group benefits can be made available to the union's members.

unisex mortality table A mortality table that shows a single set of mortality rates to be used for both males and females.

unit-benefit formula A method of calculating benefits for a defined benefit pension plan based on years of service. The formula may take into account only years of service (for example, $50 per month for each year of service) or years of service and compensation.

universal life insurance A form of permanent life insurance that is characterized by its flexible premiums, flexible face amounts, and unbundled pricing factors. For other information about universal life insurance, see also *back-loaded policy, corridor, front-loaded policy, group universal life insurance (GUL), option A plan,* and *option B plan.* See also *bundled insurance product* and *unbundled insurance product.*

universal life II See *variable universal life insurance.*

unregistered reinsurer In Canada, a reinsurer who is not licensed to accept reinsurance in a given jurisdiction. Contrast with *registered reinsurer.*

UPP See *Uniform Pension Plan (UPP).*

UR See *utilization review (UR).*

usual, customary, and reasonable (UCR) fee Under a major medical policy, the maximum dollar amount that is considered eligible for reimbursement for a given medical procedure.

utilization management A process used by many managed care plans to manage the use of medical services to ensure that the patient receives necessary, appropriate, high-quality care in a cost-effective manner.

utilization review (UR) A utilization management method intended to reduce the occurrence of unnecessary or inappropriate hospitalizations of patients. UR is generally performed by doctors or nurses who are employees of an insurer, a managed care organization, or an independent utilization review organization.

validation period The amount of time it takes for a life insurance policy to become profitable or to begin adding to surplus. Also called the *break-even period.*

validation point   The point at which a life insurance policy is neither profitable nor unprofitable. After reaching the validation point, the insurance policy begins to make a profit or add to the insurer's surplus. Also called the *break-even point.*

validation schedule   A new agent financing plan that outlines the sales (production) requirements that an agent must meet in order to continue to qualify for financing payments and, in some cases, to avoid termination of his or her contract.

valuation   The process of calculating the proper values of an insurer's assets, liabilities, and capital and surplus.

valuation actuary   An actuary who specializes in setting the proper values for an insurance company's assets, reserves, and capital and surplus.

valuation mortality table   A mortality table developed and published as an industry-wide standard for computing the values of policy reserves. Valuation mortality tables usually have wide margins of safety, indicating much higher rates of mortality than do the tables that insurers use for calculating premiums.

valuation premium   The net annual premium used to calculate reserves. The valuation premium is most often used to describe the GAAP net premium.

valued contract   A contract under which the amount of the benefit is set in advance. A life insurance policy is a valued contract. See also *contract of indemnity.*

variable annuity   An annuity under which the policy's accumulated value, and sometimes the amount of monthly annuity benefit payments, fluctuate with the performance of a separate account.

variable life insurance   A form of whole life insurance under which the death benefit and the cash value of the policy fluctuate according to the investment performance of a separate account fund. Most variable life insurance policies guarantee that the death benefit will not fall below a specified minimum. See also *investment-sensitive insurance.*

variable premium life insurance   See *indeterminate premium life insurance.*

variable universal life insurance   A form of whole life insurance that combines the premium and death benefit flexibility of universal life insurance with the investment flexibility and risk of variable life insurance. Also called *flexible premium variable life insurance* and *universal life II.* See also *investment-sensitive insurance.*

VEBA   See *501(c)(9) trust.*

vested benefit   In pension and employee-benefit terms, a benefit that a plan participant is entitled to receive if the participant leaves the plan. By contrast, nonvested benefits would be forfeited by the participant upon leaving the plan. A participant's benefits become vested after a certain number of years of participation in a plan.

vested commissions   The commissions that the insurer guarantees to pay to the soliciting agent, even if the agent's contract is later terminated. Renewal commissions are often vested.

vesting provision   A provision of an agent's contract that allows the agent to continue to receive renewal commissions and service fees for in-force policies that the agent originally sold, even after the agent has left the insurer.

vision care coverage   Insurance that provides benefits for expenses the insured incurs for eye examinations and corrective lenses.

voluntary employees' beneficiary association (VEBA)   See *501(c)(9) trust.*

voluntary plan termination   The curtailment or termination of a pension plan with the curtailment or termination being initiated by the plan sponsor. Contrast with *involuntary plan termination.* See also *distress termination* and *standard plan termination.*

voluntary termination rate   See *lapse rate.*

Voluntary Trade Association   An association composed of several employers from the same industry. Often the association will seek group insurance for the employees of its various member organizations.

waiting period   (1) In medical expense insurance, a prescribed amount of time following policy issue during which the insured's medical expenses are not covered by the policy. Such waiting periods usually last from 14 to 30 days following policy issue and normally apply only to medical expenses arising from sickness, not from accidents. (2) In disability income insurance, a specified amount of time, beginning with the onset of the disability, during which benefits are not payable. Such waiting periods may last from seven days to six months. The waiting period in a disability income insurance policy is sometimes called the *elimination period* or the *probationary period.* (3) In a group insurance plan, the length of time that a new group member must wait before being eligible to join the group plan. Also called a *probationary period.*

waiver of deductible provision   A provision found in some major medical coverages that waives a claimant's initial deductible if the claimant's medical expenses are the result of an accidental injury.

waiver of premium for disability (WP) benefit   A supplementary life insurance policy benefit under which the insurer waives renewal premiums that become due while the insured is totally disabled.

waiver of premium for payor benefit   A supplementary life insurance benefit often included in juvenile policies which provides that the insurer will waive the policy's renewal premiums if the adult policyowner, not the insured child, dies or becomes disabled.

war exclusion provision   A life insurance policy provision that limits an insurer's liability to pay a death benefit if the insured's death is connected with war or military service. See *result clause* and *status cause.*

weekly indemnity plan A type of short-term disability income insurance plan which typically pays a weekly benefit equal to a stated dollar amount or a percentage, such as 60 percent, of the insured person's earnings.

welfare benefit plan A plan or program that an employer establishes to provide certain benefits to plan participants and their beneficiaries.

well-written business Business on which (1) the specific needs of a customer have been identified by the company (or agent) and the customer has recognized that those needs are important, (2) the insurance product actually meets those needs, and (3) the customer is financially capable of paying the premiums. Also known as *quality business.*

whole life annuity A mathematical term for a series of regular periodic payments, each of which is made only if a designated payee is then alive, with the payments continuing for that payee's entire life.

whole life insurance Life insurance that remains in force during the insured's entire lifetime, provided premiums are paid as specified in the policy. Whole life insurance also builds a savings element (called the cash value). For descriptions of traditional whole life products see *continuous-premium whole life insurance, graded-premium whole life insurance, joint whole life insurance policy, limited-payment whole life insurance, modified-premium whole life insurance,* and *single-premium whole life insurance.*

with benefit of survivorship See *benefit of survivorship.*

withdrawal Voluntary termination of an insurance contract by the policyowner. See also *lapse.*

withdrawal charge A charge imposed when a contractowner withdraws more than a certain amount of money from a deferred annuity's accumulated value in one year.

withdrawal fee An amount that a customer must pay if the customer withdraws part of the account value from a financial product within a given period after purchasing the product.

withdrawal provision A policy provision that permits the policyowner to withdraw money from the policy's cash value or accumulated value. This provision is often included in universal life policies and deferred annuity contracts. Also known as a *partial surrender provision.*

withdrawal rate See *lapse rate.*

withholds Percentages of a physician's compensation that are withheld each month throughout a health maintenance organization's (HMO's) plan year and then used at the end of the plan year to offset or pay for any cost overruns for referral or hospital services.

WLC See *supplementary contract with life contingencies (WLC).*

WOLC See *supplementary contract without life contingencies (WOLC).*

workers' compensation Government-mandated insurance that provides benefits to covered employees and their dependents if the employee suffers job-related injury, disease, or death.

worksheet See *underwriting worksheet.*

WP See *waiver of premium for disability (WP) benefit.*

YBE See *Year's Basic Exemption (YBE).*

yearly renewable term (YRT) insurance Term life insurance that gives the policyowner the right to renew the coverage at the end of each year. This renewal right continues for a specified number of years or until the insured reaches the age specified in the contract. Also called *annually renewable term (ART) insurance.*

yearly renewable term (YRT) reinsurance A type of reinsurance in which the ceding company purchases yearly renewable term insurance from the reinsurer for the total net amount of risk of a block of policies. Also called *risk premium reinsurance (RPR)*. See also *net amount at risk.*

year of service As defined by ERISA in the United States, a 12-month period during which an employee completes at least 1,000 hours of service to the employer. See also *hour of service.*

Year's Basic Exemption (YBE) As defined by the Canada Pension Plan (CPP) and Quebec Pension Plan (QPP) in Canada, the first 10 percent of an employee's annual earnings up to the amount of the Year's Maximum Pensionable Earnings (YMPE).

Year's Maximum Pensionable Earnings (YMPE) In Canada, the maximum amount of employment earnings that, after deducting the Year's Basic Exemption, can be used to determine an individual's benefits under the Canada Pension Plan and Quebec Pension Plan. The YMPE is adjusted annually according to increases in wage levels.